# Gender and Caring

# Gender and Caring

## Work and Welfare in Britain and Scandinavia

EDITED BY
CLARE UNGERSON

HARVESTER
WHEATSHEAF

New York   London   Toronto   Sydney   Tokyo   Singapore

First published 1990 by
Harvester Wheatsheaf
66 Wood Lane End, Hemel Hempstead
Hertfordshire HP2 4RG
A division of
Simon & Schuster International Group

Typeset in 10/12 pt Times
by Keyset Composition, Colchester

Printed and bound in Great Britain by
Billing and Sons Ltd, Worcester

---

*British Library Cataloguing in Publication Data*

---

Gender and caring: work and welfare in Britain
   and Scandinavia
   1. Great Britain. Welfare work.   Role of women
   2. Scandinavia. Welfare work.   Role of women
   I. Ungerson, Clare
   361.3′088042

   ISBN 0-7450-0342-7
   ISBN 0-7450-0808-9 pbk

---

1 2 3 4 5   94 93 92 91 90

# CONTENTS

# ACKNOWLEDGEMENTS

Considerable thanks are due to a number of people, not least the authors of these chapters who have waited patiently during a protracted editing process. Special thanks are due to Arnlaug Leira, who visited the United Kingdom during 1988 and with whom I was able to discuss, at length and most usefully, a number of issues raised in this book.

# CONTRIBUTORS

*Anette Borchorst* is currently Associate Professor at the Institute of Political Science at the University of Aarhus, Denmark. She has worked in feminist research since 1977, concentrating on aspects of the sex segregation of the labour market and of unemployment, both private and public care work, women and the welfare state, motherhood and child care politics.

*Janet Finch* is Professor of Social Relations at Lancaster University. She has published widely on gender issues in social policy and sociology, and also on methodology. Her most recent book, *Family Obligations and Social Change* (Polity, 1989), is linked to her research on family responsibilities for supporting adult relatives.

*Arnlaug Leira* is a Senior Research Fellow at the Institute for Social Research, Oslo, Norway. She also teaches at the Oslo School of Early Childhood Education. Her most recent publications examine the relationship between the welfare state and working mothers.

*Hazel Qureshi* is a Research Fellow in the Hester Adrian Research Centre, at the University of Manchester. Her work in the field of social care has included both practice and research. She is currently working on a study of the family care of adults with mental handicap and severe behaviour problems.

*Birte Siim* is Associate Professor at the Institute of Social Development and Planning at Aalborg University, Denmark. She has researched and written on feminist theory and on women's relation to the welfare state. She is currently working on a research project on gender, power and democracy – women's citizenship in the Scandinavian welfare states.

*Clare Ungerson* is Reader in Social Policy at the University of Kent, Canterbury, England. She has written widely on women and social policy, and on sex, gender and informal care.

*Kari Wærness* is Professor of Sociology at the University of Bergen, Norway. Her research has covered the areas of social policy and family sociology, with particular emphasis on the work of women, and the relation between unpaid care in the family, and the formally organized health and social services.

# CHAPTER 1

# INTRODUCTION

CLARE UNGERSON

The papers in this volume are the outcome of a conference held at the University of Kent in April 1985. The initial purpose of that meeting was to bring together academics from the countries of Scandinavia and Britain who had for some time been studying and theorizing on the concept of 'care'. It was clear before the conference took place that in these two parts of Northern Europe, there had been certain similarities in the development of perspectives on caring. For a start, most of the academics writing on the subject, whether Scandinavian or British, were women, and based their analysis on a loyalty to and inspiration from their respective national women's movements. In other words, academic feminism, loosely defined as a woman-centred and woman-directed perspective on knowledge, had provided the context in both geographical areas for the development of the study and analysis of caring. Second, since we shared a feminist perspective it was hardly surprising that, in certain respects, our work had focused on similar topics and used similar methods of analysis. In both countries there was a recognition that the activities of the state in general and the direction of the social policy in particular were of vital importance in determining the circumstances under which 'caring' took place and the sex and working conditions of those who carried out the tasks of caring. Given a feminist perspective and the importance which feminists have attached to the use of women's experiences and their feelings about those experiences as a route to greater understanding of social processes ('the personal is political'), it was also hardly surprising that in both sets of countries, much of the feminist writing on caring was concerned to legitimate feeling as an important perspective on caring (Holter, 1984). Finally, there was also a consensus that, despite the close affiliation of the term 'caring' to feelings of affection and love, the actual process of caring constituted *work* and that that work, particularly if it took place in the home, was invisible (Wærness, 1978).

However, as emerged at the conference, there were – and are – interesting contrasts in the way thinking about caring has developed in, on the one hand, Scandinavia and, on the other, Britain. The most important difference between the discussion of 'caring' in all the Scandinavian countries and that which takes place in Britain is that, in the countries of Scandinavia, no distinction is made between 'caring' for dependent people who are not children, and caring for children. In other words, academic commentary on caring in these countries is *assumed* to entail discussion of policies for the care of normal children. In contrast, in Britain, the use of the word 'caring' is assumed to *exclude* discussion of policies for child care and is used only to refer to caring for people who are dependent, not because they are infants, but because they have some distinguishable disability. (The reasons for this difference in the range of discussion are in themselves interesting and illuminating and are discussed much further in Chapter 2 and, later, in the conclusion to the book as a whole.)

Secondly, the countries of Scandinavia, particularly Denmark and Sweden, are generally acknowledged to have developed 'welfare states' based on similar principles and which, increasingly, are unique to those countries. The central concept is one of 'citizenship' entailing rights rather than responsibilities, and an assumption that the way in which those rights can and must be satisfactorily underwritten is through state action. Moreover, Sweden in particular has developed social and labour market policies which have the explicit aim of equalizing relations between men and women (Scott, 1982) and the other countries of Scandinavia, particularly Denmark, have been heavily influenced by these policies. Moreover, it is now accepted that while post-war social policy in Northern Europe has generally differed in its fundamentals from social policy in North America and that the term 'welfare state' which is commonly applied to Britain and the Scandinavian countries has had some meaning in that sense, it is also now clear that despite the similar nomenclature, Britain's 'welfare state' has always been somewhat different from the Scandinavian model. This is particularly so in the treatment of women and especially in the assumptions embedded in social policy about the nature of family life and the marriage relationship. The chapters in this volume demonstrate some of these differences between Britain and Scandinavia, embracing as they do comparative discussion of policies for child care (Chapters 7 and 8) and pointing up differences in policy development for women and children between Britain and most of the countries of Scandinavia (Chapters 5 and 8). However, the elision of all the Nordic countries into the portmanteau of 'Scandinavia' in turn overlooks some of the contrasts between those countries. As both Borchorst (Chapter 8) and Leira (Chapter 7) point out, there are differences between them, particularly in the development of child care policies, which mean that in some respects Norwegian policies for women as mothers and workers bear a closer resemblance to British policies than they do to comparable policies in Denmark and Sweden.

There are, of course, considerable similarities between all these countries of Northern Europe, including Britain, when it comes to consideration of social and economic trends. They all share ageing populations, high divorce rates, low birth rates, and relatively high and increasing female economic activity rates which are partially and importantly generated by demand for labour in the social services. Indeed, female participation rates in Sweden, Denmark, Norway and Finland are now the highest in the developed capitalist world (OECD, 1988a, and see Chapter 7, this volume). Certain other social trends are shared by some countries and not by others: Britain and Denmark have relatively high unemployment rates for both men and women and both countries have, in recent years, experienced right-wing reforming governments. While all the countries spend large proportions of their Gross Domestic Product (GDP) on social and public services and income transfers, Britain spends 45 per cent compared to Sweden's 60 per cent (OECD, 1988b). All the countries have a women's movement, although in the countries of Scandinavia, with their long history of Social Democratic governments and corporatist traditions, the position of the women's movement within national politics is a far more integrated one than in Britain. Indeed, as far as Britain is concerned, it is no longer possible to identify a single 'women's movement' although feminism, as a mode of analysis, is far from dead, particularly in the world of universities and publishing. As far as social policy is concerned, all these countries share an anxiety about the future of care for the elderly, and in all of them policy is increasingly orientated towards maintaining the independence of old people in their own homes and away from institutions for as long as possible (see Wærness's paper in this volume).

The chapters in this book consider many of these contrasts and similarities (e.g., Chapters 5 and 8), but all share the common purpose of putting women centre-stage. As is always the case when social policy is discussed in relation to women, the interdependency of the public world of policy with the private world of care becomes the central issue. Many of the papers point out how the organization of public services plays a determining role in the way women experience some of the most important aspects of their lives – the bearing and rearing of children (Chapters 7 and 8) and the care of dependent elderly people (Chapters 4 and 6). Not all the papers have very specific policy recommendations, but those that do fall into two categories: some of the papers, particularly those from Scandinavia, look to the organization of the state and the further insertion of women into the political process in order to develop social policy that more nearly reflects the needs and aspirations of women and which counterbalances the patriarchal tendencies which are evident in even the most enlightened Scandinavian governments (see Chapter 5). Others, especially from the United Kingdom, discuss the kinds of demand which feminists, largely outside the purview of government, should make of governments when it comes to the organization of care for the elderly (Chapters 2 and 3).

While it is possible to claim correctly that feminist analysis always puts women centre-stage, this is about as far as any generalization about feminism can go, since, after twenty years of second-wave feminism, it is not really surprising that there are considerable differences between different kinds of feminism and feminist. Some of these differences are addressed in the chapter by Janet Finch where she reviews the 'liberal feminist' or 'equal rights' position on community care (so far the only moderately successful feminist action on community care in Britain) and finds it wanting. Both Finch and Ungerson, in their chapters in this volume, address the question as to what might be a wider agenda for feminists of a more radical turn of mind, with Finch querying the concept of 'community care' altogether, while Ungerson (somewhat reluctantly) suggests that equal pay for caring work (rather than equal rights for carers) might be one way forward.

One central issue that is implicit in many of the chapters and explicitly mentioned in some of them (Chapters 2 and 6) is the question of how far the argument that much of 'caring' is work should be taken when it comes to remuneration, and, most particularly, professionalization. There is a strong strand of feminist writing that argues that historically, particularly in the feudal period, women's skills as carers in general, and health workers in particular, were widely recognized and respected (see, for example, Ehrenreich and English, 1976). Feminists tend to argue that with the development of capitalism and industrialism, and the rise of a male-dominated medical profession, those caring skills that women contain and maintain from generation to generation have been down-graded to the extent that they are now either treated with hostility – 'old wives' tales' and the persecution of midwives – or simply ignored altogether. Some of this kind of argument is referred to in some of these papers, namely, that women do have caring skills and successfully deliver very considerable quantities of welfare to numbers of dependent adults and children; the problem is that these skills remain unrecognized. The difficulty is that, as the state withdraws more and more from the direct provision of care, particularly for the elderly, it now has an interest in ensuring that this apparently spontaneous caring by women is organized on a predictable and mass scale. There seem to be only two ways of doing this: either attempt to introduce into existing or newly built residential areas elements which will encourage such caring spontaneity, or borrow professional values from the world of well-paid work – of therapy, the monitoring and evaluation of outcomes, and the equitable and efficient distribution of caring resources between dependent people with similar needs – and try to 'manage' spontaneity. A 'community care industry' filled with case managers, social planners, community development workers, architects and town planners and even public relations officers, is growing up before our very eyes. Feminists are right to be wary of these developments; they are clearly the front line in a move to professionalize 'caring', develop hierarchies and bureaucracies and, in so doing, create a niche which men can all too easily fill (Hearn, 1982). There is therefore a tension between the need to recognize the caring skills which women already contain and pass on, through socialization into femininity, to the next generation of women, and the need to develop decent remuneration for personal service work, with all that seems to entail in terms of training, credentialism and hierarchy. That tension and contradiction is not resolved within the pages of this volume; it clearly needs further thinking about.

British readers may be surprised to learn that the Scandinavians are concerned about the development of state patriarchy (see Chapters 5 and 8). In some respects the welfare systems of Scandinavia, particularly Sweden and Denmark, seem so deter- minedly gender-free compared to that in Britain that it is rather strange to discover that some of the same feminist critique can be applied to Scandinavian welfare states. However the emphasis of the critique is rather different. The British feminist critique of the British welfare state tends to focus on its in-built sexism particularly in the assumptions about the sexual division of labour embedded in the social security system, and in the personal social services as they apply to community care. Moreover, the critique also argues that the way in which people's lives develop is less and less dependent on the delivery of welfare by the state; the state itself sees the family as the lynch-pin of welfare delivery systems. The Scandinavian critique tends to stress the central issue of the dependency of women on the operation of the welfare state rather than on the family or the labour market. Once women are the consumers *par excellence* of welfare state services and their position and life experience as paid workers, mothers, and carers hinges crucially on the way in which those services operate, it clearly becomes absolutely essential that women's needs are taken into account at every twist and turn of the political process. It therefore becomes possible to argue that, given the welfare state's centrality in the delivery of welfare in the countries of Scandinavia, such political representation of women's interests that there is does not adequate- ly reflect the great importance of the state's activities in determining the quality of women's lives. So long as the public world of politics remains relatively male-dominated, there lurks a danger that the enormous strength of the state could be turned against women.

The book is organized in the following way: the first four chapters are by British authors (Ungerson, Finch, Qureshi) and they, largely, consider issues particularly relevant to debates and re- search on community care for the elderly in Britain. The following chapter by Birte Siim is a comparative discussion of the politics of the development of services in relation to women in Britain and Denmark. Kari Wærness critically assesses the assumptions that surround the debates concerning the dependent elderly in the countries of Scandinavia, particularly Norway. Arnlaug Leira looks at the other kind of 'care-work' considered in the Scandinavian literature – that of the care of children, particularly pre-school children – and the way in which pre-school day care has (and has not) reflected the need to draw women into the labour market. Anette Borchorst further considers the development of provision of policies for the care of pre-school children, providing a comparative account of Britain and Scandinavia. Clare Ungerson brings the book to an end with a brief conclusion which brings together some of the strands of the book, and criticizes present political developments in Britain which bear some parallels with Scandinavian developments, but which, she suggests, are being worked out within a very different context.

# References

Ehrenreich, Barbara and English, Deidre (1976), *Witches, Midwives and Nurses: A history of women healers* (London: Writers' and Readers' Publishing Co-operative)

Hearn, Jeff (1982), 'Notes on patriarchy, professionalisation and the semi-professions', *Sociology*, vol. 16, no. 2, pp. 184–202, excerpted in Clare Ungerson (ed.), *Women and Social Policy: A reader* (London: Macmillan)

Holter, Harriet (ed.) (1984), *Patriarchy in a Welfare Society* (Oslo: Universitetsforlaget)

Organisation for Economic Co-operation and Development (OECD) (1988a), *Employment Outlook* (Paris: OECD)

Organisation for Economic Co-operation and Development (OECD) (1988b), *OECD Economic Surveys: United Kingdom* (Paris: OECD)

Scott, H. (1982), *Sweden's 'Right to be Human': Sex-role equality – the goal and the reality* (New York: M. E. Sharpe, Inc.)

Wærness, Kari (1978), 'The invisible welfare state: women's work at home', *Acta Sociologica*, supplement, pp. 193–207

# CHAPTER 2

# THE LANGUAGE OF CARE
## Crossing the boundaries

CLARE UNGERSON

## Talking about 'care'

There are always many reasons for holding cross-national discussions and conferences in the field of social policy, not least the camaraderie and the feeling of international solidarity that almost always occurs. But the more intellectual intention is that we will learn from each other new ways of practice and of thinking. There is no doubt that the study of policies elsewhere can sometimes lead to innovation and change in the practice of policy at home, and, if it does not, can more clearly reveal the structural differences between nations and societies which act to prevent such direct cross-fertilization. In any event we should come away from the experience with a deeper understanding of our own society. Similarly, the study of policy discussion and debate in other countries can reveal different ways of thinking which in turn can clarify and develop policy debates at home. In this chapter I am going to look at the latter of these aspects of comparative work and suggest that feminist debate about caring has been helped, in Scandinavia, by the development there of a language with which to discuss caring in all its forms and wherever it takes place and which speaks more directly to feminist analysis. Moreover, I shall go on to suggest that this rather different language in itself makes it possible to consider policies which, until now, have been very little considered within the British feminist literature (except by Hazel Qureshi whose chapter in this volume tackles many of the same issues but with a somewhat different emphasis), and which, at the end of this chapter, I argue should be discussed openly and seriously – although always within a broad feminist framework.

It was striking at the conference that the Scandinavians were surprised by the very specific meaning attached to the words 'care', 'carer' and 'cared for' by the British participants. In the countries of Scandinavia, as we shall see later, this kind of language is applicable to many different kinds of servicing by one individual for another irrespective of whether such servicing is paid for, and/or carried out in an institutional or familial setting, and irrespective of whether the care is for a very young or very old person, a very ill and abnormally dependent person or, simply, an immature person – i.e. a normal child. In Britain, the term 'caring' and the noun 'carer' have come to refer to a very specific kind of relationship between, usually, two people, one of whom is highly dependent and usually adult, and the other of whom looks after the dependent person and does it 'at home' and for no pay. Sometimes – but by no means always – this kind of 'caring' is distinguished as 'informal care' while other kinds of service carried out for similarly dependent people, particularly that provided by the statutory social services and voluntary agencies within both domiciliary and institutional settings, are distinguished as 'formal care'. The implication is that informal care which takes place in the private domestic domain, is spontaneous and hence unplanned, unregulated and unobservable. It is based on obligations founded on feeling and affiliation, rather than on the rationality and detection of 'need'. 'Informal' care is assumed to be restricted to one-to-one relationships, where one person provides continuous and twenty-four-hour care, on an apparently unchanging basis laid down by feelings of love and duty. In contrast 'formal' care, which takes place in the public domain, is provided by large numbers of substitutable social service personnel to even larger numbers of clients on a basis of affordable cost, and competition between clients. 'Formal' domiciliary services are provided usually for only a small part of the twenty-four-hour day, and, reflecting the general division of labour amongst health and social service personnel, only for very specific tasks. In theory, at least, the provision of such formal services continues only so long as the allocators of services consider that the costs of providing services are balanced by the benefits derived therefrom (efficiency) and that there are no more pressing claims, based on 'need', elsewhere (equity).

## The public/private split: a false dichotomy

This conceptual splitting of 'formal' from 'informal' care follows the conceptual split between 'public' and 'private' spheres – a division which itself has been criticized by British and American feminists for underplaying the way in which the two spheres interrelate and interdepend. Perhaps because the word 'caring' has slipped into the British vernacular to refer largely to the *informal* caring which – by definition – only exists within the private domain, it is noticeable that the British feminist literature on caring has tended implicitly to accept the conceptual division between public and private and stress the private context of caring. 'Carers' are generally regarded by feminists, just as much as by policy-makers, as very similar to mothers and housewives, working in their own homes and providing services for close kin. In other words, the world of 'caring' in the British sense is assumed to be filled with women carers who are looking after their own kin at home. As far as the state in general is concerned, and policy-makers in particular, the problem they then have to grapple with is how to guarantee this care by women and maintain its continuity despite social trends, such as the increasing propensity of women to work in the labour market, which tend to absorb much of women's time (Moroney, 1976). Within the feminist tradition, the predominant form of analysis of this kind of care is to look to the literature on housework and child care – two activities often described under the generic term 'domestic labour'. That literature looks at the sexual division of domestic labour (for example, Witherspoon, 1985, and many others), the circumstances under which it is carried out (Oakley, 1974), and the psychological effects on the housewife (Gavron, 1968). Drawing on this largely feminist literature, much of the analysis of caring then devolves into a study of the sexual division of the labour of caring at home (Wilkin, 1979; Nissel and Bonnerjea, 1982), a consideration of the circumstances under which caring labour is extracted within the private sphere (Finch and Groves, 1983; Ungerson, 1987) and the effects on the informal carers' finances and morale (Baldwin, 1985; Glendinning, 1983).

Both policy-makers, commentators on caring, and even feminists, then, find themselves dealing with a central problem in the use of the word 'care'. The contemporary assumption is that the chief locus of love is the domestic hearth. Thus the location of the tasks of 'caring' within the domestic domain in itself means 'caring' as an activity is also assumed to constitute a set of feelings between people which are appropriate to the private, rather than the public, sphere. In other words, the word very effectively elides the twin ideas of 'labour' and 'love' (Graham, 1983). Not only that; given its location within the private sphere, the loving elements of the word 'care' can easily assume pre-eminence over its labouring elements. It is then an easy step not only to presume that such care, based on affection, is qualitatively different from the rationality-based 'formal' care but, because of the loving feelings contained within it, it is *better* care. (See Hazel Qureshi's chapter in this volume for a critique of the work of Philip Abrams who argued this point of view.)

For policy-makers this is no problem. In periods, such as the one Britain is at present experiencing, of radical changes and reductions in the public sector provision of care (Griffiths, 1988), the claim that care by close kin at home is better care is a very convenient one. A recent very glossy publication put out by a public relations firm to describe the steps being taken to close down Canterbury's local mental hospital is called *Coming Home*. On the cover two photographs, one in black and white of a long, empty and forbidding corridor at the hospital, and one in colour of a young couple holding hands and walking their dog through a sunlit field, convey the message that care at home is peopled by those who love you and it brings colour and companionship back into your life.

For feminists, however, the use of the word 'caring' to refer to activities in the domestic sphere, rather than in the public sphere, creates problems. First of all, if one argues, as most feminists of whatever politics do, that domestic labour is essentially exploitative of women then the word 'care' has to be extended beyond its conventional meaning to convey that exploitative element. But 'care' has acquired such an overlay of the feelings of affection and continuity that it turns out to be very difficult to do this. In an early attempt to find a new and more accurate vocabulary, Parker suggested that the word 'tending' might be more suitable in order to convey the work involved (Parker, 1980). More recently Land and Rose have used the expression 'compulsory altruism' to convey the additional element of constraint on choice, and, ultimately, exploitation of women (Land and Rose, 1985). Neither phrase seems to me to be wholly satisfactory. Although the word 'tending' is intrinsically a good one since it denotes work and could be equally applicable to the public and private spheres, it does not seem to have been widely adopted nor does it convey the element of exploitation; and while the linking of the word 'compulsory' with the word 'altruism' draws attention, through the phrases' very contradictoriness, to the public world of rules and regulations and the private world of unconditional giving, it is too general to denote the particularity of 'caring'. I myself have argued that we have to be clear whether we are talking about 'caring for' someone in the sense of doing the work of looking after them, and 'caring about' someone in the sense of loving them (Ungerson, 1983). In this sense, 'caring for' someone could equally well be carried out in the public as well as the private domains. But even this splitting of the word 'care' into its two separate elements seems to me to be somewhat misleading, since, in common parlance, we just as often use the term 'care for' to convey affection – as in 'I care for you' meaning 'I like you'.

Secondly, despite Hilary Graham's most fruitful and illuminating article pointing out the need to analyse the 'labour' and 'love' of care together (Graham, 1983), British feminists still face the problem that the term 'caring' with its overlay of meaning to do with affection and spontaneity is largely used to describe relations within the private sphere, while the public sphere of caring is all too easily treated as the place where skill effectively acts as an exhaustive surrogate for love. In effect, British feminist commentators find themselves having to grapple with a conceptual dichotomy between public or 'formal' care on the one hand, and private or 'informal' care on the other, when it might be rather more illuminating to consider the two contexts of care together and understand their similarities and differences by analysing them together. One might then be able to discuss, for example, the question of working conditions, remuneration, skill, and division of labour within the context of informal care just as much as within formal care. These questions tend to be unasked – certainly by British feminists – and are in the process of being pre-empted by researchers who, in evaluation of new developments in the remuneration of community care 'helpers' who are neither wholly voluntary nor paid the rate for the job, do not use a feminist framework (for a further discussion of Challis and Davies (1986) see pp. 17–22). Similarly, we have a somewhat attenuated literature on the way in which feeling in general, and love in particular, can and does enter the 'formal' domain of care. Only the work by Hazel Qureshi (see Chapter 4) really tackles these kinds of similarities between formal and informal care in practice, although in a recent exhortatory and idealist book, Gillian Dalley argues that within a general socialist transformation of society, it would be possible to develop collective forms of care which copy some of the best and most 'caring' elements of informal care, while, at the same time, avoiding its burdensome and ultimately exploitative elements (Dalley, 1988).

All this kind of analysis might be assisted if only we had a word or phrase, in the English language, that was equally appropriate to the work of caring within the public and private domains and which made it possible, without going into contortions of definition and always returning to first principles, to think about labour and love in both contexts. The consequences of doing so should be far-reaching; without pre-conception that 'love lies at home; therefore home is best' or 'institutions institutionalize' or 'collective care is non-exploitative care', we could begin to consider more fruitfully the exact circumstances – formal or informal – under which caring labour is exploited labour, the exact circumstances – formal or informal – where it is labour willingly and/or lovingly given, and the exact circumstances – formal or informal – under which the best possible standard of care, combining continuity, consistency, and respect between carer and cared for, can be provided. If such conceptual bridge-building could take place, then it might be rather more easy to consider feminist forms of care where the analysis does not counterpose so-called community care as essentially sexist and residential care as potentially non-sexist (see Finch, 1984). Indeed, it might be possible to develop an analysis which proposes policies containing elements of both public and private domains (i.e. love and labour, wages and psychic rewards) and evaluates them using the same criteria.

## A Scandinavian understanding

It should be fairly obvious by now that, in contrast to the British, the Scandinavians appear to have shaped not only a vocabulary, but also a mode of analysis which crosses the public/private conceptual division and allows them to analyse aspects of the two domains together. The major innovator in this respect is the Norwegian sociologist Kari Wærness, one of whose papers is published in this volume. In a paper first published in English in 1984, Wærness suggests a typology of care which dissolves the distinction between public, or formal care, and private, or informal care, by concentrating on the power relationship between carer and cared for, and on the actual work involved (Wærness, 1984).

In that paper, Wærness argues that there are three different kinds of care: personal services, care-giving work, and spontaneous care. Each of these different kinds of care denotes a different kind of relationship between carer and cared for (although she does note that there can be overlaps between the three which can give rise to some definitional problems). *Personal service* care is characterized by an unequal relationship between carer and cared for, where the cared for person is of superior social status to the carer. Moreover, the services rendered by the carer are services which the cared for could provide for themselves and, if relations between them were symmetrical, would indeed do so. Such services, Wærness suggests, are typically provided by women for their husbands, their older children, and other adult members of the family, and consist of such mundane tasks as fetching slippers and making coffee. Although Wærness herself does not make this clear, such personal service care can be equally well carried out in the context of paid work (by, for example, domestic servants) as in unpaid work. In contrast, *care-giving work* is characterized by a relationship between carer and cared for where the cared for, through illness, handicap or youth, is incapable of self-care, and hence is in a position of dependency and helplessness *vis-à-vis* their carer. This kind of care is characteristically consistent and reliable. Once again, it is possible to use this kind of definition of caring within both public and private domains, and within the world of paid and unpaid work (nursery nurses, mothers caring for their own infants). Finally, there is what Wærness calls *spontaneous care*; this differs from care-giving work precisely because it is not consistent and reliable, but arises impulsively and spontaneously. Wærness suggests that this kind of care can particularly arise in some communities, where neighbours can offer each other impulsive services without a risk of incurring an expectation of continuity. Once again, it is possible to imagine spontaneous care arising within paid work, where the workplace itself acts as a kind of community and provides a context for the development of occasional acts of caring (covering for someone who is ill or depressed, looking after a work-mate's child).

Clearly these distinctions are not wholly straightforward, and there are certain objections that can be made about them. For example the boundaries between the different kinds of care could change over time, such that, for example, if someone chose to manipulate a carer spontaneous care could, over time, become personal service care; similarly, there may be difficulties in making absolute distinctions between personal service care and care-giving work, particularly between kin where power and status relations and, most particularly, the degree of accepted legitimate dependency, are – sometimes – open to negotiation. But what is important is that these distinctions between different kinds of caring break down the dichotomy between paid, formal, caring and unpaid, informal, caring. As Wærness says:

> The dimension private–public is not a clear-cut dichotomy. It is a dimension referring to how particularistic the care-giver is allowed to be in her distribution of help and support. (p. 74)

In other words, according to Wærness' formulation, 'private' care is care that is given on an individualistic basis, whether or not the carer is paid for her work and whether the payment, if it is made, comes via public funding or from the person being cared for. The phrase 'allowed to be' implies that in 'private' care the care-giver is relatively free to decide how and when to do the care-giving work. 'Public' care is care that is provided on a collective basis, where carers, operating within an occupational and usually professionalized and highly structured hierarchical division of labour, provide care for a large number of 'clients'; while this kind of care is generally paid for, whether through public or private funding, it can equally well be provided by volunteers working in voluntary organizations.

This is not just another way of dividing up knowledge and making an already somewhat confused vocabulary even more complicated. These new distinctions between different kinds of caring, characterized by the basis of the relationship between carer and cared for, by the power relationship between the individuals involved, and by the degree of autonomy of the care-giver means that not only can conceptual breakthroughs be made, but there are also important policy implications. Most important of all, given that these different kinds of care can take place in both public and private domains, it means that the affective portion of the word 'care' – its loving elements – are subordinated to the *tasks* involved in the *work* of caring. This emphasis on the labour rather than the loving elements of caring is particularly brought out in Wærness' term 'care-giving *work*' which she uses to describe the care of people (adults and children) who cannot look after themselves and who are in a position of great dependency on the person looking after them. A most important conceptual and policy consequence follows: if caring is fully recognized as work, irrespective of the context within which it takes place, then the questions as to whether or not caring should be paid for, at what rate, and operated under what working conditions, can be considered with much greater clarity. If, using the Scandinavian tradition and language, we accept that 'care-giving work' – defined as Wærness suggests to refer to the individualistic relationship between carer and cared for – takes place in both the 'formal' and 'informal' caring domains, then we can begin to compare the rewards, working conditions, and exploitative elements of those two domains. Arguing for equity between them, we can begin to suggest how and why remuneration for the work done and compensation for exploitation should be calculated – *on the same basis* – in both domains. In other words, we can begin to consider why and how caring, in whatever context it occurs, should be waged.

## Existing payment for care-work in Britain

The question of paying all carers irrespective of the domain in which they work is not entirely unrealistic, especially since certain developments of paid care in the domestic domain are currently taking place in Britain. Diana Leat and Pat Gay, in their study *Paying for Care* (1987), have described and discussed the rapid, haphazard and relatively undocumented development of paying 'ordinary people' to provide caring services in Britain. In their study Leat and Gay concentrate on the provision of care by carers who typically provide quasi-fostering services in their own homes for highly dependent people (e.g. the frail and confused elderly, the mentally and physically handicapped) or highly disruptive people (e.g., disturbed teenagers). The research report raises a series of questions about the meaning and function of payment for such caring, the relationship between the carer and the paying authority, and the relationship between this kind of payment and the wages paid to more conventional 'employees' which are highly pertinent to this chapter. However, the authors remain somewhat undecided as to whether such schemes are exploitative of carers, although they do discuss the question at length and in a most interesting and useful way. As will be made clear in this discussion, I am of the opinion that these forms of payment *are* exploitative of carers' labour and – given that these 'ordinary people' are almost always women – depend on the continued general subordination of women in British society.

In order to consider the question of exploitation and relate it to the more general question of whether 'informal' carers should be paid, I shall consider below one of the best-known – because it is exceptionally well documented – paid care schemes (see Challis and Davies, 1986). This is the Kent Community Care scheme (also described by Hazel Qureshi in her chapter in this volume) which is at present only available for the very frail elderly who are almost always resident in their own homes. The people included in these schemes are normally very highly dependent and selected on the basis that if such care were not provided, they would have to be permanently resident in a relatively costly old people's or nursing home.

The paid carers in the Kent Community Care scheme are known as 'community care helpers'. Typically, they work outside office hours, getting the elderly people for whom they care up in the morning, securing their safety and nourishment during the day, and finally getting them to bed in the evening. The assumption is made that these are tasks that can be bounded and defined, and the workers are paid an individually assessed amount for each visit made to the elderly person they care for. The number of visits made bears little relation to the amount of time actually spent with the elderly person, and, as Challis and Davies themselves point out, one of the advantages of the scheme is that helpers can themselves choose to spend as much time with the person they care for as they desire, or deem necessary. At 1977 prices, the average amount paid for each visit was £1.75 (Challis and Davies, 1986, p. 127). Thus a helper who visited an elderly person twice a day, once in the morning to get her out of bed, make her breakfast, and settle her in an armchair for the day, and again late at night to put her to bed and give her a nightcap, would earn, if this occurred every day including weekends, £24.50 a week. However, the basis on which such community care helpers are paid is still in the process of evolution.

In the Kent Community Care Scheme, no two helpers received the same amount and, indeed, at an early stage in the scheme, a number of 'helpers' were providing their contracted services for free (Qureshi, Challis and Davies, 1989). Their remuneration was assessed according to the personal circumstances of the care-giving worker and how far payment would take her beyond tax and social security thresholds (see p. 22, below), the degree of dependency of the old person and difficulty in caring for him or her, whether the helper provided whole-day and/or whole-night support, and whether the old person moved into the helper's household (Challis and Davies, 1986, p. 128). The one principle that is maintained rigidly in this scheme is that the helpers are *not* paid for the time they spend with the old person, but rather for the tasks they are contracted to carry out and the number of visits they make. They therefore received no pay during holidays or sickness. This complete lack of employment rights seems to have been somewhat diluted in subsequent copy-cat schemes (Challis, Chessum, Chesterman, Luckett and Woods, 1987, p. 19). Leat and Gay, in their description of the payment of carers in quasi-fostering schemes, which arguably demand even more of the carers in terms of time, begin one of their chapters on 'Exploitation, payment, and rationality' with an invented advertisement:

> Wanted: mature, tolerant, 'warm' applicants (with a sense of humour) for demanding job. Knowledge and experience required. Hours as necessary but on call for 24 hours, 7 days a week. No fixed term of employment, irregular, unspecified periods of work and payment – but applicants must demonstrate long-term commitment/ availability. No national insurance, no pension, no paid holidays. Applicants must be able to provide (extra) accommodation and meet all expenses incurred. Pay – around 50p per hour (minus expenses). (Leat and Gay, 1987, p. 59)

In the Kent Community Care scheme, and presumably in other schemes, community care helpers have sometimes been recruited from existing informal carers (Challis and Davies, 1986, p. 120). In other words, the schemes can and have been used to pay care-giving workers for the work that they have been conventionally providing for free. The circumstances under which such informal carers have been recruited have varied: in the Kent scheme, for example, informal carers have been paid enough to prevent them going out to another kind of paid work, or, informal carers have been persuaded that their change of status to that of 'community care helper' providing delineated services through contracted 'tasks' would limit the amount of caring they felt they had to provide for their dependent elderly kin (Challis and Davies, 1986, p. 120). (However, see Hazel Qureshi's chapter in the present volume for an indication that the idea that this would impose a limit on the amount of work the helper was expected to give did not at all work out in the way initially expected and the caring relationship broke down.) Whatever the basis on which such informal carers have crossed the boundary from totally unpaid care-giving work to nominally paid care-giving work, two important points remain. First, they demonstrate that under certain circumstances, the British state, in the form of a few local authority social service departments, is beginning to pay care-giving workers irrespective of the domains in which they operate. Second, however, it is also clear that as these schemes are developing at the moment, they are hardly designed to emphasize the work element of 'care-giving work'; rather they seem designed to bring into the more formal domain the affective and loving elements assumed to be part of 'informal' care but assumed to be *missing* from 'formal' care. In other words, the conceptual boundary between the 'formal' and 'informal' worlds of care-giving work is being strictly maintained and reinforced. Instead of emphasizing the *existing similarities* between work in the two domains and then considering how that might be best rewarded and remunerated on an equitable basis, proponents of these kinds of scheme argue that very small payments for work carried out provides the basis for the *transformation* of so-called formal relationships into 'informal' – and hence better – relationships between carer and dependent. Moreover, it is assumed that 'informal' care contains the affective elements that, in their turn, are assumed to be missing from 'formal' care. Challis and Davies, using work originally carried out by Hazel Qureshi and described at greater length in her paper in this volume, reveal these implicit assumptions in their description as to how these changes come about.

*Client–helper relationships: the shift towards informal care*
The social workers saw helpers as having a separate and distinct contribution to make to the care of the elderly. It was not simply care to meet basic instrumental needs of daily living, however important

this was, but care with an affective basis which in many respects resembled that of informal care . . . interviews with helpers who had been involved with a client for a considerable time indicated that the importance of the contract had diminished. For these people, a relationship had developed with the elderly person whom they helped and the tasks and activities undertaken had broadened out, albeit within the original planned approach.

The development of this relationship, where the original formal approach grew into a personal exchange between helper and helped – in short the move towards informal care – could be observed in four ways. First, helpers undertook tasks which were not required in the original contract. They tended to do more and different tasks for their clients. Second, helpers developed strong attachments to individual clients and were unwilling to change, even when for other reasons this might have been convenient for them. People would retain contact with clients even after leaving the scheme. Third, in many cases a feeling of personal responsibility emerged, a feeling which some helpers likened to their responsibility for dependent members of families such as children. Fourth, helpers with families tended to involve them in looking after the elderly person. Husbands would do odd jobs in people's homes, young children visited and elderly people were taken for meals to helpers' homes. (Challis and Davies, 1986, p. 142)

It is undeniable that a number of very frail elderly people have benefited considerably from these schemes, and that, in a few cases, their informal carers have also been relieved of full-time care by the provision of the services of a 'community care helper'. The moving case-studies in Challis' and Davies' book, plus the quantitative documentation of improvements of morale, testify to this. However, the success of such a scheme, at least in financial terms, is predicated on the recruitment of casual, rightless and exceptionally cheap labour. By re-emphasizing and re-formulating the boundary and differences between 'public' and 'private', 'formal' and 'informal', such schemes make two implicit assumptions. First, that full and proper payment for care within an organizational hierarchy effectively *excludes* the more affective and loving elements of care, and secondly, that it is not only possible but it is morally *right* to recruit workers who are willing to work unsocial hours for very little pay. The assumption is that nominally paid workers will provide better-quality care since they are doing the work for love rather than money, although the payments in themselves mean that the workers will provide a consistent and continuous service based on a binding contract.

The first assumption is a very sweeping judgement of the nature of care-giving work in the more 'formal' sector: personal attachment to clients almost certainly develops in the formal, more public, domain and as Hazel Qureshi points out in this volume there is evidence from a number of studies to indicate this. There is no logical reason to assume that a full-time home-help will never invite a client to her home for Christmas lunch, or that care-giving workers in residential homes will not develop deep feelings for and provide high-quality 'extra' services for many of the people whom they look after. In other words, the important point made by Wærness and developed by others – namely, that care-giving work in both domestic and more formal domains can and does consist *both* of labour *and* of love – is, by schemes such as these, implicitly and totally denied. This is logically absurd and empirically unfounded. Such assumptions certainly need testing.

Secondly, and just as importantly, such schemes are intrinsically based on an assumption of the continuing subordination of women. It is no surprise to learn that in the schemes about which most of the research has been published, namely in Kent and Gateshead, 94 per cent of the helpers in the first Kent scheme were women (Challis and Davies, 1986, p. 124) just as in Gateshead 'most' of the helpers were women (Challis *et al.*, 1987). There are two reasons for this predominance of the female sex: the job description and the selection process, and the exceptionally low pay. At the initial selection interview for helpers, certain points were made, for example, 'in those cases where the individual's need and desire for a regular wage clearly outweighed their interest in work with the elderly, it was usually agreed to proceed no further.' (It is interesting to note that there seems to be an assumption implicitly stated here that 'work with the elderly' is completely incompatible with a 'regular wage'.) 'The team had few initial preconceptions about the attributes of a suitable helper, save a caring attitude and sound commonsense'; 'the previous caring experience of the potential helper, whether on a formal employed basis or informal basis, was considered particularly important.' (Almost two-thirds of the helpers recruited in the first Kent scheme had at one time worked in the female-dominated service sector as nurses, care attendants, home-helps and other social service workers.) Clearly, helpers were expected to be predominantly women and it followed that the vast majority recruited were women. But this, in itself, could create problems since women, typically, are the focus and locus of a whole network of emotional and servicing relationships within the family: 'Potential external constraints which could impinge on the ability and willingness to help were also explored during the initial interview. It was possible that family relationships, especially the attitude of the husband, could be strained by the wife engaging in new activities of her own . . . in some cases, it was only the payment offered by the scheme that made helping legitimate in the eyes of husbands, although this was not a prime reason for the wife's involvement.' (All quotes taken from Challis and Davies, 1986, pp. 121–2, *passim*.)

In describing the system of payment for the helpers, Challis and Davies discuss a number of criteria used for judging the appropriate fee per visit (see above, p. 18). It is clear that one important basis in assessing payment for the care of each particular elderly person was the financial circumstance of the helper; payment seems to have been deliberately kept below tax and social security thresholds:

> The payment system represented a clear example of one of the many constraints facing innovation, namely the powerful pressure to conform to the requirements of existing structures. It required a great deal of liaison and negotiation with other departments of the local authority and an acquisition by the team members of detailed knowledge of National Insurance, taxation and benefit thresholds which could influence helpers' payments. (Challis and Davies, 1986, p. 128)

Thus the tax and social security systems, both of which, in Britain, are notoriously discriminatory against women (Land, 1983), and which are a very important determinant of the economic position of women within the family and of the incentives for women to enter the labour market, were being used to delimit the rate at which individual helpers were to be paid. While I suspect this was no conscious decision on the part of the scheme managers, the already highly structured and subordinate position of women within British institutions was no doubt an added convenience in keeping the overall costs of the scheme relatively low.

The way the payment system worked strongly echoes Laura Balbo's argument in her essay 'Crazy quilts: rethinking the welfare state debate from a woman's point of view' (Balbo, 1987). In that article Balbo suggests that 'the fragmented pattern of provision of goods and services is an institutionalized characteristic of late capitalist societies' (p. 64) and that women make their way through this system by 'patching and piecing' as though they were making a patchwork quilt:

> Looking at different countries or even a single country, over a period of time, one finds that state policies are used very flexibly. Services which were at one point delivered by the state – through nursing homes for the elderly, or mental hospitals, for instance – are being devolved to the community using unpaid family or volunteer work . . . I would argue that nothing inherent in any specific service explains the particular historical way in which the service itself is delivered: *rather, logic and interests that are generated at other levels of the social and economic system account, partly at least, for any particular choice in its mode of delivery.* In all cases . . . women's servicing work is required, interchangeable (provided within families, through state agencies, by the market according to changing requirements), flexible, cheap. *And servicing provides not only a huge amount of work, at little or no pay; most importantly, it represents women's ingenuity in the innumerable concrete ways of piecing and patching resources, their understanding of and response to personal needs, and their ambivalence in dealing with the prevailing rules. Quilt-making is women's work, with little exception* [my italics]. (Balbo, 1987, pp. 65–6)

I am reminded of one of my own students who was a helper on the Kent Community Care scheme and who used the money to top up her grant and pay for petrol to get to the University. She enjoyed the work she did on the scheme and the company and conversation of the person she looked after, but finally something had to be sacrificed in her busy day and she found she had to leave the University for a year.

This long critique of a form of payment for 'private' care-giving as it is developing in Britain at the moment is intended to illustrate two points: first, the boundary between so-called paid formal care and unpaid informal care has already been breached by the British state. Secondly, this scheme is precisely what I do *not* have in mind when I suggest that feminists should begin to consider, as a general policy for the development of caring which is not exploitative of the unpaid labour of women, the payment of so-called informal carers. This is because I have argued that schemes like the Kent Community Care scheme pose a false dichotomy between the 'formal' and 'informal' spheres of care by assuming that the nature of the relationships that prevail in each one of these spheres is totally different; in the one, they seem to argue, loving relationships prevail to the exclusion of all other considerations, and in the other, monetary, contractual and bureaucratic relationships prevail and love and spontaneity are absent. As Hazel Qureshi's research has convincingly demonstrated, the signing of a contract to carry out certain tasks of care can and usually does become an irrelevance in caring relationships. As I have argued earlier in this chapter, the important contribution to thinking about caring that has come from Scandinavia and particularly in the work of Kari Wærness, is the argument that all caring is work, irrespective of the domains in which it takes place, and that payment for it does not necessarily and in itself alter the nature of the relationship between carer and cared for, since the chief dimension along which caring and servicing relationships are determined and should be analysed is that of *power*. Moreover, love can be combined with paid labour – or, to put it another way, there is no reason to think that, if the morale of paid workers is high and

**Table 2.1** Working conditions – formal and informal care.

| Formal care | Informal care |
| --- | --- |
| Division of labour | Very limited division of labour depending on provision of support services |
| Dispersed responsibility | Total responsibility |
| Limited working hours | 'On call' at all times |
| Substitutability and cover when ill | No substitutability or cover when ill |
| Multiplicity of clients | Very few clients (usually only one) |
| Social networks with other workers at workplace | No social network at workplace; possible isolation |
| Potential for economic and union organization at workplace | Limited potential for organization and only through political process |
| Accountability and hierarchy | Almost complete autonomy |
| Waged | No payment, except through benefit system |

they are relatively autonomous in the work they do, that they will not offer precisely the kind of additional caring services which Challis and Davies assume is part only of the so-called informal sector of care. Secondly, I have argued that such schemes are predicated on the assumption of the continued subordination of women in British society; they implicitly assume that there is a pool of labour available that is willing to be casually employed, with hardly any employment rights and at a rate of pay that bears little or no relation to payment for similar work carried out by fully contracted workers. And they also implicitly assume that such 'helpers' will be willing to work at such low rates of pay because they are engaged in a lifelong process of 'piecing and patching' and the putting together of a package of resources for themselves – the structure of which is already largely pre-determined by the essentially sexist tax and social security systems that exist in Britain.

## A basis for comparison

Let us now turn to consider the equitable basis on which payment for care-giving work could be calculated. First it is necessary to describe the working conditions that prevail within the so-called formal and informal domains. A rather stylistic and over-simplified typology of difference and similarity can be devised, as shown in Table 2.1.

It should be stressed that this typology applies only to working conditions, and not to the nature of the relationship between carer and cared for. Using the Wærness formulation, it is just as possible to carry out 'care-giving work' within the formal as the informal sector since in both places care of a particular nature and from one individual to another takes place. The major difference in the formal sector is that the person doing the care-giving work has to distribute her services between a number of clients in a similar situation, whereas in the informal domestic sector (except where a spouse is caring for a spouse) the carer typically distributes her services to a number of people within her household whose circumstances differ; in the domestic domain, she divides her time between care-giving work and what Wærness calls 'personal services' to other people within her household (see Ungerson, 1987, for a description of the competition for the services of a carer within the domestic domain).

This typology suggests that there are large differences between the working conditions of the people carrying out care-giving work in the formal and informal sectors. In general the working conditions of carers in the formal sector are rather better than those in the informal sector. Formal carers have the benefit of the opportunity to form social (and economic) relationships with fellow workers; they can benefit from the division of labour in the form of shared responsibility for the welfare of their clients and a limited working day. If they are ill they need not feel obligated to carry on working since they can be confident that their labour can and will be replaced – and if it is not the resulting difficulties are the responsibility of the organization rather than their own. The major drawbacks for formal carers are that they may find themselves subject to demands from multiple clients, and can have considerable personal and professional difficulties in satisfactorily working out priorities. Secondly, they may feel that the division of labour is, in the classical Marxist sense, alienating. While it implies shared responsibility (which might be something of a comfort when dealing with seriously ill and chronically dependent people) the division of labour may also mean that they feel deprived of autonomy and the ability to treat the 'whole' person in a satisfying way. And last but not least, they are paid for the work they do – not necessarily a great deal, but at rates of pay generally negotiated between their employers and large and relatively powerful political and economic institutions – namely, the carers' trades unions (in Britain these are the various doctors' and nurses' associations and unions, plus the Confederation of Health Service Employees (COHSE), the National Union of Public Employees (NUPE), the National Association of Local Government Officers (NALGO), and the British Association of Social Workers (BASW).

In contrast, the working conditions of carers in the informal sector are less good. The work is generally in very isolated conditions, such that carers in these circumstances report considerable loneliness (see, for example, Ungerson, 1987). There are very limited opportunities for contact with fellow-workers for either economic or social reasons (in Britain the growing network of carers' support groups and the establishment of the National Association of Carers may do something to alleviate this but these organizations are probably only in contact with a small proportion of carers and, anyway, do very little to alleviate carers' day-to-day isolation). Informal carers experience very little division of labour, and, if they do receive support services, it is generally their responsibility to organize their receipt, to ensure that they arrive and to wait until they do so (waiting, and being subject to the working routines and regimes of others, is one of the problems British informal carers frequently report). Informal carers are therefore on call most of the day and night, and, particularly if the caring takes place in their own home, they may well have difficulties asking someone to substitute for them since this entails an invasion of privacy and a possible threat to their property. But just as there are some disadvantages of the division of labour in the formal sector (see above) so there are some advantages to be derived for the informal carer who works alone: she is 'her own boss' and can and does decide how best to organize the work; the work is not alienating, at least in the classical Marxist sense, since she can treat the 'whole' person and see the immediate outcome of her work. But, last but not least, in Britain at any rate, she receives no payment for the work carried out; at best she receives a payment from the state – the Invalid Care Allowance – which is no more than a nominal recognition, not of the work carried out, but of the time spent which might otherwise be used to generate an income from waged work.

It is these comparisons of working conditions in the two domains in which 'care-giving work' takes place that persuade me that there is at the very least a strong case for arguing that all care-giving work, including that normally called 'informal care' in British parlance, should be waged. If care-giving work is to be paid for, assessment of the 'rate for the job' should be based on three principles: equity of treatment between 'formal' and 'informal' care-giving work, equal pay for equal work, and compensation for unpleasant or difficult working conditions. It should immediately be obvious that payment for carers in the informal sector would be greater than payment for those in the formal sector, in order to compensate informal carers for their isolated working conditions, and pay them for their undivided responsibility. However, the fact that formal carers have rather less autonomy in their work acts as a counterbalance and should decrease the pay differential between the two kinds of carer a little. I have also quite deliberately omitted mention of payment for being 'on call'. Given the twenty-four-hour nature of the work for most informal carers, the amount of pay that they should rightly get if all these hours were taken into account, combined with compensation for sole responsibility, would almost certainly mean that informal care would become prohibitively expensive, and all care would be transferred to the formal sector for pure cost reasons, rather than considerations of what is the most appropriate form of care for the dependent person and their relatives. The chief principles on which such payment would be based differ fundamentally from the assumptions embedded in schemes such as the Kent Community Care scheme. First and foremost such payment should be based not on an assumption of the *difference* between the two spheres of caring in terms of the kind of relationship that prevails within them, but rather on the *similarities* of the *work* involved.

## Wages for caring?

There is no denying that payment for domestic labour, of which 'informal' caring is a part, is problematic and proposals for and against payment for all or parts of domestic labour have been much discussed by feminists over this century. In the first wave of feminism there were fierce arguments, particularly among socialist feminists, as to whether it were better to provide for mothers and their children through cash payments to the mother or rather through social services designed to relieve mothers of at least some of the work of child care (see, for example, Neild Chew, 1913, for a discussion of the early twentieth century situation and Hilary Land, 1975, for a historical account of the debate earlier this century concerning family allowances). More recently similar debates emerged in British feminism in the 1970s and have re-appeared again in the late 1980s. The more recent discussion became known as the 'domestic labour debate' and a campaign for 'wages for housework' was mounted by some British feminists (see, for example, Malos, 1982; Fairbairns, 1979). These ideas are critically referred to by Janet Finch in her chapter in this volume where she argues that such payment may lead to the further entrapment of women in domestic labour.

I have considerable sympathy with this critical argument partially because it is possible that payment for caring will actually make the position of carers in the domestic domain worse: it might be suggested that if some one individual is being paid to do the care-giving work then it is unnecessary for there to be many – or any – support or substituting services. And yet it is the nature of much caring work that it is extremely demanding particularly because it asks for not just physical labour but emotional labour as well. Indeed when informal carers are interviewed about their lives and how they might be improved, they often refer to the need for relief – in other words, that someone or something should temporarily substitute for their labour. (In Britain, various systems of relief have evolved: day hospitals, day care, respite care, sitting services, etc.) However, if 'informal' carers were paid, such relief might be less forthcoming on the assumption that the payment of an individual to take *chief* responsibility also entails *sole* responsibility. (But then this assumption hardly differs from the *de facto* position that exists for most unpaid carers at present.) In contradiction to this argument is the suggestion that if carers were paid there would have to be at least an implicit if not an explicit contract for the tasks they are expected to undertake and that this would put boundaries around their responsibilities.

Some of the anxieties of the commentators concerned about a possible decrease in the quality of care should so-called informal carers be paid have already been discussed and I have suggested that these worries largely arise out of a false dichotomy they draw between the nature of relationships that prevail in the public world of 'formal' care and the private world of 'informal' care. Moreover, as Hazel Qureshi points out in her article in this volume, the payment of carers, if only as helpers on the Kent Community Care scheme, does have effects on the relationship between carer and cared for, but these effects are complicated and almost all of them to the good. It can make the person being cared for less anxious about being a burden because the pay acts as a surrogate for the reciprocity which they themselves are unable to offer; it can generate care that would otherwise be unavailable since the kin of the dependent person, due to the particular emotional dynamics between people who have known each other for many years, may be quite unable to offer caring services. Indeed, if 'informal' carers were paid there is no necessary link between kinship and informal care, since the motivation to care would be generated not only by the rules of gendered kinship (see Ungerson, 1987), but also by the income that would be available for the work undertaken. In other words, paid informal carers might just as well be intimate strangers as intimate kin; if carers come forward not because they are driven to do it through an overwhelming sense of duty, but rather because they perceive it as a job that combines monetary reward with public recognition and the satisfaction of providing services for those who need them, the quality of care might well improve.

One further argument against payment must be mentioned, partially because it has appeared in the feminist literature, not least in Kari Wærness' work. This is that there are dangers in developing a system of care that lends itself to bureaucratic and state control, and which, in itself, may decrease versatility and worker autonomy both of which qualities, in the complicated business of caring for the very dependent, are highly desirable. In other words, the heavy hand of the contracting employer may lead to the development of cautious hierarchies operating in a rule-bound and over-professionalized world. This is a danger which must be acknowledged, just as the great advantage of schemes like the Kent Community Care scheme – namely, their versatility – must also be acknowledged. But it still does not seem to me that there is a logical connection between very low pay and versatility and imagination on the one hand, and reasonable pay and bureaucratic strangulation on the other. As Kari Wærness herself said at the conference in 1985, no one ever suggested that a much-liked and competent male professional should be paid *less* because he is more 'caring'.

The tension and contradiction between these arguments for and against paying carers is interesting and needs much further consideration and, if possible, empirical testing, particularly within a feminist framework. Despite the well-taken strictures from Janet Finch (see this volume) that payment to individual 'informal' carers would continue and powerfully reinforce the trend to privatize community care within the domestic domain and lead to the further entrapment of women, one can also see that such payment might provide the basis for two further developments: first, the recruitment of many more men into the role of domestic carer, and, secondly, the possible pooling of individual carers' resources such that they can use their pay to organize more collectively based services catering for groups of dependent people. This would exactly follow the way in which groups of individually contracted general practitioners working within the British National Health Service presently come together to form primary care health centres where they can substitute for each other's labour and develop extra services, thus providing a better service for their patients and an easier and more interesting life for themselves. Such group schemes, if they involved paid and heretofore 'informal' carers, could provide for a rather more genuine and potentially less sexist system of spontaneous and co-operative 'care *in* the community' than is at present envisaged.

But all these aspects of possible payment to carers entail much more careful consideration and discussion. The most important point is that the work of carers, in whatever domain, has to be recognized and, if they are to deliver high-quality services with love and respect for the people they care for, their morale must be high. This depends a great deal on their working conditions, their self-esteem, and the recognition of their work by others. If payment for 'informal' care is to occur in Britain, then the basis of the payment for that work must be founded on the assumption that the conceptual boundary between the work undertaken in the 'formal' and 'informal' domains is a false one, and the criteria for the assessment of the level of pay must be based on an assumption of the *similarities* of the work in the two spheres. Meantime, while such a long-term feminist agenda is being considered and discussed, one thing is clear: that in the short run one obvious feminist aim should be that community care 'helpers' should be paid the 'rate for the job'.

# References

Balbo, Laura (1987), 'Crazy quilts: rethinking the welfare state debate from a woman's point of view' in Anne Showstack Sassoon (ed.), *Women and the State: The shifting boundaries of public and private* (London: Hutchinson)

Baldwin, Sally (1985), *The Costs of Caring: Families with disabled children* (London: Routledge and Kegan Paul)

Challis, David, Chessum, Rosemary, Chesterman, John, Luckett, Rosemary, and Woods, Bob (1987), 'Community care for the frail elderly: an urban experiment' in *The British Journal of Social Work*, vol. 18, pp. 13–42

Challis, David, and Davies, Bleddyn (1986), *Case Management in Community Care* (Aldershot: Gower)

Dalley, Gillian (1988), *Ideologies of Caring: Rethinking community and collectivism* (London: Macmillan)

Fairbairns, Zoe (1979), 'The co-habitation rule – why it makes sense', *Women's Studies International Quarterly*, vol. 2, pp. 319–327, excerpted in Clare Ungerson (ed.), *Women and Social Policy – a reader* (1985) (London: Macmillan)

Finch, Janet (1984), 'Community Care: Developing non-sexist alternatives', *Critical Social Policy*, no. 9, pp. 6–18

Finch, Janet, and Groves, Dulcie (1983), *A Labour of Love: Women, work and caring* (London: Routledge and Kegan Paul)

Gavron, Hannah (1968), *The Captive Wife: Conflicts of housebound mothers* (Harmondsworth: Penguin)

Glendinning, Caroline (1983), *Unshared Care: Parents and their disabled children* (London: Routledge and Kegan Paul)

Graham, Hilary (1983), 'Caring: a labour of love', in Janet Finch and Dulcie Groves (eds), *op. cit.*

Griffiths Report (1988), *Community Care: Agenda for action*, a report to the Secretary of State for Social Services (London: DHSS, HMSO)

Land, Hilary (1975), 'The introduction of Family Allowances: an act of historic justice' in Phoebe Hall, H. Land, R. Parker and A. Webb, *Change, Choice and Conflict in Social Policy* (London: Heinemann), also excerpted in Clare Ungerson (ed.), *op. cit.*

Land, Hilary (1983), 'Who still cares for the family? Recent developments in income maintenance, taxation and family law', in Jane Lewis (ed.), *Women's Welfare, Women's Rights* (Beckenham: Croom Helm), also excerpted in Clare Ungerson (ed.), *op. cit.*

Land, Hilary, and Rose, Hilary (1985), 'Compulsory altruism for some or an altruistic society for all?', in Phillip Bean, John Ferris and David Whynes (eds.) *In Defence of Welfare* (London: Tavistock)

Leat, Diana, and Gay, Pat (1987), *Paying for Care: A study of policy and practice in paid care schemes* (London: Policy Studies Institute)

Malos, Ellen (ed.) (1982), *The Politics of Housework* (London: Allison and Busby)

Moroney, Robert M. (1976), *The Family and the State: Considerations for social policy* (London: Longmans)

Nield Chew, Ada (1913), 'Should wives be paid?', *The Labour Woman*, November

Nissel, Muriel, and Bonnerjea, Lucy (1982), *Family Care and the Handicapped Elderly* (London: Policy Studies Institute)

Oakley, Ann (1974), *The Sociology of Housework* (London: Robertson)

Parker, Roy (1980), *The State of Care* (Jerusalem: Joint (JDC) Israel Brookdale Institute of Gerontology and Adult Human Development in Israel)

Qureshi, Hazel, Challis, David, and Davies, Bleddyn (1989), *Helpers in Case Managed Community Care* (Aldershot: Gower)

Ungerson, Clare (1983), 'Why do women care?', in Janet Finch and Dulcie Groves (eds.), *op. cit.*

Ungerson, Clare (1987), *Policy is Personal: Sex, gender and informal care* (London: Tavistock)

Wærness, Kari (1984), 'Caring as women's work in the welfare state' in Harriet Holter (ed.), *Patriarchy in a Welfare Society* (Oslo: Universitetsforlaget)

Wilkin, David (1979), *Caring for the Mentally Handicapped Child* (London: Croom Helm)

Witherspoon, Sharon (1985), 'Sex roles and gender issues' in Roger Jowell and Sharon Witherspoon (eds.), *British Social Attitudes, the 1985 Report* (Aldershot: Gower)

# CHAPTER 3

# THE POLITICS OF COMMUNITY CARE IN BRITAIN

JANET FINCH

The focus of this chapter is the politics of community care in Britain especially as they have developed since the mid-1960s. Over this period we have experienced a series of policy initiatives which have promoted community care rather than residential care for a range of disabled, infirm and elderly people. Over the same period there has been an increased acknowledgement politically of the rights of women, stimulated in part by the so-called second wave feminism which took off in the late 1960s. How have these two sets of political changes connected with each other in relation to the role of women as providers of unpaid care for their relatives? As the politics of welfare have changed, have they in any way taken into account the issue of women's rights and women's roles? If so, in what ways and with what consequences?

With this set of questions in mind, I shall try to link the mainstream politics of community care with feminist politics over the same period. My aim is both to understand from a feminist perspective what has been happening in Britain, and also to assess the opportunities afforded within the present politics of community care for further advancing the position of women in British society.

I would like to thank Dulcie Groves and Jane Lewis. Even if they would not necessarily agree with everything I have said, they each have helped me to think through the ideas in this article in our many conversations about community care.

## Community care: developments in policy and practice in Britain

The purpose of this section is to provide an introductory account of how the policy and practice of community care have developed, especially for readers not familiar with the British scene. I shall attempt no more than an outline in this chapter, as fuller discussions are readily available elsewhere (for example, Finch and Groves, 1980; Walker, 1982; Parker, 1985; Henwood, 1986). It is of course a necessarily selective outline in which I pay particular attention to those issues which are important for feminist politics; but I believe it to be a fair account, recognizable by most commentators in the field across a broad political spectrum.

To make this brief outline a little more concrete, I will use one particular illustration, namely the care of mentally ill and handicapped people, citing especially the documents produced by the House of Commons Select Committee on this issue and the government's response to their recommendations (House of Commons, 1985; Department of Health and Social Security, 1985). I am using this illustration partly because it will help to counterbalance the tendency of many commentators in this field (including myself) to concentrate on the care of elderly people as the main example. It is also an area which brings some of the key issues into sharp focus, as is apparent in the Audit Commission's (1986) report on community care, upon which I shall also draw.

The historical account of the development of community care policies in Britain is usually dated from the 1950s, although some of the ideas which it incorporates can certainly be traced at least to the early part of this century, when recommendations were made by a Royal Commission that the 'feeble minded' (that is, mentally handicapped people) could sometimes be best cared for in a supervised way outside large residential institutions (Walker, 1982; Parker, 1985). However the first significant piece of legislation to incorporate a commitment to a policy of community care was the 1959 Mental Health Act, which covered the care of both mentally ill and mentally handicapped people. The commitment contained in that legislation was given administrative effect initially in relation to mental illness, in that the 1962 Hospital Plan proposed to halve the number of beds in large hospitals within fifteen years. The importance of the vision contained in this document, whereby out-dated and out-moded 'asylums' would be replaced by a more humane regime of care, is recognized by the recent House of Commons Report, which quotes the 1962 Plan at length. The Plan called for

> nothing less than the elimination of by far the greater part of this country's mental hospitals as they stand today. . . . There they stand, isolated, majestic, imperious, brooded over by the gigantic water-tower and chimney combined, rising unmistakably and daunting out of the countryside – the asylum which our forefathers built with such solidity. (Quoted in House of Commons, 1985, para. 14)

Whilst it was in relation to mental health that the policy of community care initially was developed, the idea that large residential institutions should be replaced by more small-scale, localized forms of care rapidly became the common currency of debates about provision for the whole range of physically and mentally handicapped and elderly people. Social scientists fuelled this debate by publication of studies such as Townsend's *The Last Refuge* (1962) which demonstrated the unacceptable reality of life in large-scale and isolated residential institutions. Other developments in policy and practice tended to give more general support by bringing the concept of 'community' to the fore, as a plank of social policy; for example, community-based projects in urban development, education, housing, and the development of community work itself. Two official reports in particular gave these developments impetus: the Skeffington Report which advocated citizen participation in planning, and the Seebohm Report on local authority social services, which believed that these should be community-based (Report of the Committee on Local Authority and Allied Personal Social Services, 1968; Ministry of Housing and Local Government, 1969).

Thus by the early 1970s the ideology of community in general and community care in particular was well established across a wide range of services but policies to implement it were still in a relatively early stage. At this time, the emphasis tended to be rather more on care 'in' the community than care 'by' the community, to use an important distinction drawn by Bayley in 1973. That is, community care policies at this stage were concerned very largely with issues of how to replace large residential institutions with smaller residential units located in ordinary surroundings, and to develop the support services to enable relatively dependent people to live lives which are as normal as possible. 'The community' was seen as the location for care, but the provision of facilities and services was still largely assumed to be the responsibility of public authorities. But during the 1970s that emphasis began to shift and by the end of the decade, care 'by' the community had become a very much more prominent feature of policy (Willmott, 1984; Walker, 1986). From a feminist perspective this was a very important shift and it is worth considering it in some detail (Finch and Groves, 1980).

The idea of care 'by' the community is distinctively different from care 'in' the community although it is a much more slippery concept. Its central implication is that some person or persons conceived of as 'the community' actually provides the care needed by dependent people – but there can be wide variations in precisely who is intended, what kind of caring should be provided, and on what terms. Its meaning, however, conveys the idea of contrasts with other types of provision: voluntary rather than statutory, informal rather than formal, unpaid rather than paid. Policies which encapsulated these shifts in policy were developing throughout the 1970s and probably found their most complete expression in a central government document on services for elderly people published in 1981. This document stresses that the care of elderly people is the responsibility of everyone, not just the government, and lays down the following principles for providing it:

> Whatever level of public expenditure proves practicable, and however it is distributed, the primary sources of support and care are informal and voluntary. These spring from the personal ties of kinship, friendship and neighbourhood. They are irreplaceable. It is the role of public authorities to sustain and, where necessary, develop – but never to displace – such support and care. Care *in* the community must increasingly mean care *by* the community. (Department of Health and Social Security, 1981, p. 3)

The economic reasons for these shifts are all too obvious: the 1970s was of course the decade in which public expenditure contraction began in earnest in Britain and other western countries, and in addition policy-makers became acutely aware of the rising cost of providing traditional residential care which was bound to accelerate the search for alternatives (Walker, 1982). But whatever the underlying reasons for these policy changes (an issue to which I return in the next section) by 1980 not only had community care become firmly fixed as a central theme in the development of social services, but increasingly it meant that public services themselves should no longer be fully and directly responsible for providing care; indeed their role was increasingly being seen as limited to co-ordination of services provided by voluntary organizations, volunteers, friends and relatives (Walker, 1982; Parker, 1985).

The question of who provides the front-line care was often left rather hazy in these statements but it has become increasingly clear that all the evidence points to the family of the dependent person, especially those sharing the same household as the people who carry most, often all, the burden – a point that is now widely acknowledged (Parker, 1985; Henwood, 1986). The feminist critique of community care policies dates from this time, when it was becoming all too obvious that community care in effect meant family care, which in turn meant care by women often with little practical support from elsewhere (Finch and Groves, 1980). The only financial support available for people who take on this work of caring for their relatives, the Invalid Care Allowance (ICA) introduced in 1975, at that stage was not available to married women who formed the great majority of such unpaid family carers (Groves and Finch, 1983).

In the 1980s the policy of community care has become consolidated in its meaning of 'by the community' and represents a consensus across all political parties about the way forward for the provision of social care services. Indeed, in a sense it fits well with the more general concept of the 'mixed economy' of welfare which has increasingly become the political orthodoxy in the 1980s; that is, the idea that welfare provision should properly comprise a mixture of services, some provided by the state, some by the private market, some by voluntary and charitable organizations and some through so-called informal means. In relation to the community care of dependent people the idea of 'interweaving' statutory, voluntary and informal care became the keynote (Henwood, 1986).

From the point of view of the family members – largely female kin – who provide the 'informal' part of the care, their participation had become consolidated as a central and desirable feature of care provision, with other services in a sense merely supplementary. The permanency accorded to family care has been acknowledged in the concern which grew in the middle of the decade about the need to 'support the carers' who had hitherto often been carrying the burden unaided. But other than the expansion of carers support groups (many of them self-help and voluntary in character), at the time of writing there is little evidence that this support is going to take concrete and practical forms (Henwood, 1986). In terms of financial support for carers, the ICA was extended to married women in 1986, following a ruling of the European Court of Justice on a case brought by a British woman, Jacqueline Drake (Szysczak, 1987). These developments are important from the perspective of the feminist politics of community care and I shall discuss their implications more fully in a later section.

At the same time as the idea of community care has become firmly entrenched as the orthodoxy at the level of rhetoric and policy intention, in the 1980s there has been increasing evidence that developments in practice do not match the rhetoric. In terms of financial support for carers, the major changes in social security legislation introduced in 1986, which in principle provided a significant opportunity for a government committed to supporting carers to extend benefits available to them, are if anything likely to have the effect of making the situation worse (Family Policy Studies Centre, 1986; Land and Ward, 1986). In relation to domiciliary services and other forms of practical support for dependent people living in their own homes, there is evidence that the level of provision remains poor and inadequate to meet demands, especially so if the person who needs care lives in a household with other adults (particularly women) when these adults are often unobtainable (Parker, 1985, pp. 68–9). Moreover in many instances a policy of developing community care has meant that the cost of services is simply shifted to a different sector of public expenditure. Many people who once would have been cared for in local authority homes and long-stay hospitals are not living independently 'in the community' but in private residential homes, with their accommodation costs funded through the social security system (Audit Commission, 1986).

There is a very real sense, then, in which the idea of community care has become meaningless. The gap between intention and practice is too wide in many cases to say that we have a 'policy' of this kind at all; the range of services which can variously be put under this heading is so diverse as to make the term useless as a description; and the use of 'community care' as a concept has shifted so fundamentally from care 'in' the community to care 'by' the community to the interweaving of statutory, voluntary and informal services, as to make it useful only as a means of obscuring the real issues rather than illuminating them. All of this was well recognized by the House of Commons report on community care of mentally ill and mentally handicapped people, which concluded that the phrase 'means little in itself' and that it might be more helpful to abandon it (House of Commons, 1985, para. 11). That report also highlighted the way in which the headlong rush into community care policies for mentally handicapped and mentally ill people – especially the pressure to close large hospitals without first developing adequate alternative provisions – has resulted in the gap between rhetoric and reality being so wide as to be a parody of a community care policy. Perhaps the ultimate irony is that there is a danger that many more people suffering from mental illness and incapacity will end up in the 'care' of the prison service, having committed criminal offences in 'the community' and there being no other places where they can be securely contained (para. 161). The report concludes that the impetus to develop community services was essentially seen as a way of saving money, but that this logic is fundamentally flawed – good community services are likely to be more, not less, expensive than the residential hospitals which they replace and without additional resources some very vulnerable people will find themselves discharged from hospital into a completely inadequate alternative:

> We are at the moment providing a mental disability service which is under-financed and under-staffed both in its health and social aspects. Proceeding with a policy of community care on a cost-neutral assumption is not simply naïve: it is positively inhumane. Community care on the cheap would prove worse in many respects than the pattern of services to date. (House of Commons, 1985, para. 21)

A similar theme was echoed, again with a high level of concern expressed, in the Audit Commission's report. In relation to services for mentally ill and mentally handicapped people, the report notes that there were 37,000 fewer patients in hospitals in 1985 than a decade earlier, but that no-one knows what has happened to many of those who have been discharged. Information is not available which would indicate what kind of support (if any) they are receiving 'in the community'. Drawing on research in America they warn:

> If recent US experience is any guide, it is likely that a significant proportion of those discharged will have been before the courts and will now be imprisoned; others will have become wanderers, left to their own devices with no support from community-based services. (Audit Commission, 1986, p. 18)

In summary, by the middle of the 1980s the policy of community care had become firmly established and commanded a broad political consensus in terms of rhetoric.[1] The particular form which it now takes emphasizes the provision of care by non-statutory services, in the context of the mixed economy of welfare. There are, however, grounds for serious doubts about the effects of the policy in practice. Those doubts can arise very clearly in the case of mental illness and handicap services because people are actually being discharged from long-stay hospitals, and a direct before-and-after comparison can be made. In the case of services for elderly people the issues are less visible because, rather than the movement of people out of residential care, the pressure on community-based services comes from increased demand created by rising numbers of elderly people in the population. But the underlying question is the same: does the policy of community care deliver adequate services in practice? The authoritative answer given by the Audit Commission (1986) is that at the moment this is not happening.

## The politics of community care: competing accounts

What are the underlying political and economic pressures which have brought about British community care policies in their present form? Why have the policies outlined in the previous section developed in the ways described? Clearly there are a number of demographic and economic pressures which have brought about these changes, and which have occurred in countries other than Britain. But unless we are going to consider them as simply a pragmatic set of responses to pressures outside the control of governments, we have to ask whether these policies have an overall coherence at the political and ideological level. In other words, is there really a guiding rationale, whether overt or covert?

The existing literature on community care offers various versions of the guiding rationale for community care policies. I shall begin by contrasting two which suggest very different accounts of what such policies are 'really' about. The first of these I shall call the 'naïve official account'. This account runs like this: the replacement of out-dated and inhumane residential institutions with the opportunity for people to live independently in the community was the action of enlightened governments acting in the interests of handicapped and elderly people themselves. We now realize that it is much better for even highly dependent people to live as normal a life as possible, and the development of community care policies represents the means for securing that end. Statements to this effect can be found in successive official documents and reports; for example the following selection:

> The sense of belonging to a family may be of great importance to the patient. It is not always in his best interests to remove him to even the best-run foster home or public institution. (Report of the Royal Commission on Mental Illness and Mental Deficiency, 1957)

> The aim of the government's policies is to enable elderly people to live in their own homes wherever possible – which reflects what the majority themselves want. (Department of Health and Social Security, 1981, p. 6)

> Community care is a matter of marshalling resources, sharing responsibilities and combining skills to achieve good-quality modern services to meet the actual needs of real people, in ways which those people find acceptable and in places which encourage rather than prevent normal living. (Department of Health and Social Security, 1985, para. 3)

In so far as such policies do meet real needs, respond to popular demand, and enable people to live normal, independent lives there would seem to be little grounds for opposing them and it is easy to see why they command such wide support. However, doubts about whether the actual practice meets those aspirations in most cases must raise questions about whether policies of community care have actually been introduced for reasons solely, or even centrally, to do with the needs and demands of those who require it. It is interesting that the 1985 House of Commons Report found that no-one who submitted evidence was 'opposed to the basic principles of community care' but at the same time, the committee heard 'a chorus of deeply felt anxieties, protests and fears' about the implementation of these policies and the inadequacies of facilities for mentally handicapped and mentally ill people to be cared for outside of hospital settings (House of Commons, 1985, para. 28). Such protests indicate that, if indeed the policies have 'really' been about providing a better and more humane standard of care, their implementation has been seriously flawed.

It is not difficult to see why most people would reject this particular account of policy developments, seeing perhaps most obviously a desire to save public money as a particularly clear ulterior motive. Feminists in particular would argue that what we see here is a clear attempt to shift the burden of resources for providing care from the public purse to the unpaid labour of women who care for their relatives. This leads me to the second account which I want to contrast with the first and which I shall call the 'crude feminist account' of community care policies. That account runs as follows. In a period when governments are trying not only to reduce public expenditure but also to deal with the problem of unemployment, encouraging women to take on the unpaid care of their own relatives provides a neat solution to a number of problems. Women are forced out of the labour market and back into the home, thus accomplishing the following: costs of caring on the public purse are reduced; jobs are released for male workers and the unemployment totals go down; the home is confirmed as women's rightful place and therefore men's dominant position is maintained (but of course women will be allowed out again in the future if their labour is needed). An additional twist would be added by some feminist commentators, who argue that all of this represents a back-lash against the limited gains which women did achieve in the 1960s and 1970s;

> The Thatcher philosophy attempts to provide an ideological legitimation for both the attacks on women that result from the recession and for policies that take those attacks even further . . . a recession encourages the development of a right-wing anti-feminist revival. The idea that women should accept that their place in society is to be at home caring for their family appears to make more sense to more and more people when jobs are scarce. (Gardiner, 1983, p. 195)

There is more than a hint in this particular account of a conspiracy against women formed by the interests of men, of capital, and of the state which represents both. I have, as I indicated earlier, deliberately over-drawn both these accounts to highlight the contrast between them, but the crude feminist account which I have presented has the appeal of all conspiratorial accounts in its simplicity and directness and many feminists are undoubtedly attracted to it. However, I would argue that, just as it is easy to see why the 'naïve official account' should be rejected, or at least modified and qualified, the 'crude feminist account' is inadequate for similar reasons: the world is just not that simple. Whilst it is certainly true that community care policies have the convenient dimension that (if they are successful) they may reduce the numbers of people looking for paid work, the pressures which have produced them and shaped them in their present form amount to more than this simple equation. Further, as I shall argue in the next section, this same set of policies which has effectively sought to confine women to the home has at the same time taken some account of women's demands and women's needs. The idea of the straightforward conspiracy does not quite match the evidence.

There is therefore more to understanding how and why community care policies and practices have developed in their present form than either of these two contrasting accounts suggests, although both contain an element of truth: if it works well, community care may indeed offer a more satisfying and independent life to handicapped or infirm people than any of the alternatives previously on offer; it may well also do that at the expense of women whose unpaid labour provides family care. Self-evidently, a more complex account of the underlying rationale is needed. What should the major element of that account be? In my view, to understand the social-political and economic pressures which have produced the policy and practice of community care described above, we need to see this as a set of interwoven pressures, most but not all of which have been pushing in a similar direction.

First and most obviously there is the desire to save public money which I referred to above. Notwithstanding the evidence that little money may be saved in practice, this represents a major rationale for community care. 'Saving money' in this context of course means that contraction comes in those resources which are channelled through government and local authorities, but it may not necessarily mean that fewer resources are actually put into the care of elderly and dependent people: as feminists in particular have argued, community care policies do not look like a cheap option if one counts in the unwaged labour of women (Nissel and Bonnerjea, 1982; Rimmer, 1983; Finch, 1986). Quite apart from that, the cost of providing various domiciliary and other back-up services for dependent people living outside residential institutions may well exceed the cost of the residential institutions themselves – a point made forcibly by the House of Commons Committee in its recommendations that 'the Government [should] now accept that genuine community care policies are achievable only in the context of some real increase over a period of years in expenditure' (House of Commons, 1985, para. 21; see also Audit Commission, 1986). The Government's response to this distances it from a crude money-saving rationale but emphasizes that resources have to be used 'responsibly';

> The aim is not to save money but to use it responsibly. What we cannot afford is to waste resources on buildings, land and services which have increasingly little relationship to needs and priorities, and which make increasingly small return in quality of service. (Department of Health and Social Security, 1985, para. 4)

Second, demographic change, and especially the rise in the numbers of elderly people in the population, has made it seem particularly urgent that alternatives to existing provisions were found for this group. In common with most western European countries, the proportion of elderly people in the population has been rising and will continue to rise to the end of the century. Most importantly, the most rapid rises will be in the oldest sectors, that is, those most likely to need caring services. Whilst the projected rise in the population aged 65 and over is 7 per cent, the expected rise for those in the over-75 age group is 31 per cent and in the group over 85 it is 90 per cent (Family Policy Studies Centre, 1984). This means that, even if all facilities existing in the 1960s had been maintained, there would be substantial under-provision of traditional residential care for elderly people now and to the end of the century. There is also some evidence that there has been an increase in the overall numbers of physically and mentally handicapped people surviving into adulthood, following advances in medical technology (Parker, 1985, pp. 11–13).

Third, the left-wing critique of welfare which developed

from the 1960s onwards focused upon the repressive and controlling potential of welfare provision, perhaps most obviously in the radical social work critique (Bailey and Brake, 1975). Combined with the existing critique of residential institutions, much of it also produced by people who were themselves politically left of centre, this led to pressure for more client autonomy and even control over services and for their de-professionalization. In the context of these particular political ideas, 'community' provision of services means control and self-determination by service users, which can mean something very different from other versions of 'community care'. In practice, however, the use of the same phrases and some of the same ideas has tended to line up left-wing opinion with the other political interests on this issue.

Fourth, and coming from the opposite end of the political spectrum, the image of 'community' can be seen as part of reactivating a political agenda which values the traditional locality, its stability, its inclination to self-help, and its basis in family ties. Writers who adopt this perspective on community care tend to be much more explicit about the role of the family (which they regard as paramount) and indeed these policies align well with a renewed emphasis on 'supporting the family' as a central aim of social policy. This view has certainly been reflected in official documents on community care. Increasingly from the mid-1970s onwards, as Parker notes, policy documents were seeing families as the frontline carers as a matter of policy (not just as a matter of fact) and the role of statutory services was seen principally as supporting them (Parker, 1985, pp. 4–5).

The pressures which have produced community care policies cannot therefore be reduced to a single explanation but are centrally concerned with managing economic and demographic change. The political climate which has fostered them arises from a rather curious alignment of right-wing and left-wing agendas around the idea of community care.

How far, and with what consequences, have feminist politics entered this scene? Whilst many of the changes described above have certainly worked against women's interests and I remain convinced that their net result is bad news for women (Finch, 1984), I would argue that the feminist critique of these policies specifically, and more generally the activity of feminists and advances in women's rights over the same period, have themselves constituted another source of pressure which has shaped community care policies and practice. Whilst the pressures for change which I itemized above have tended to push in the same direction (although not always uniformly) feminists have offered an alternative view which sounds a more jarring note. In particular, I would suggest that the feminist critique has been responsible (not alone, but as an important element) for making visible the unpaid work of people who care for their relatives, for insisting that policy-makers take account of that work as part of their calculations and for questioning the terms, both financial and practical, upon which women (and to a much lesser extent men) carry out this work. Certain changes which have taken place in the 1980s in the emphasis of community care policies can indeed be seen as responses to this agenda: in particular, the new emphasis on 'supporting the carers' and the limited increase in women's financial entitlement represented by the extension of the Invalid Care Allowance to married women.

Of course there are no grounds for seeing these as significant and dramatic gains: the government had to be squeezed hard in the European Court before it gave way on ICA, and so far as 'supporting the carers' is concerned, it can also be seen as a policy which will encourage more people to take on these tasks, and to continue them for longer once they have started, thus reducing demand for other services and helping to reduce the cost on public resources. Whilst I do not think that feminists should have any illusions about these changes, they do nonetheless represent gains for those women who currently are providing unpaid care for their relatives, and more generally an extension of women's rights, and in my view there is no virtue in failing to recognize those few gains which have been made. I would argue that the pressure which eventually forced the government to give way on ICA was inspired by the feminist critique and action in a general – and to some extent in a direct – way. The demands of women to be given equal access to this financial benefit were accorded a legitimacy which they would not have enjoyed a decade earlier – indeed this was not considered an important issue in 1975 when ICA was first introduced. Conversely, the government's continued opposition began to look very unreasonable by the mid-1980s given the apparent commitment of successive governments to give women and men equal rights, as I shall argue in the next section. In a slightly different way, the insistence of feminists on making carers visible has at least contributed to the pressures which are currently generating policies for their support.

Thus the monochrome picture of community care policies as a conspiracy against women needs to be replaced by an understanding that change is not always uniform and in which, whilst many changes may indeed be against women's interests, some gains can be and have been made.

## Feminist politics and the community care agenda

What kind of gains do these changes represent for women? Are they a victory for the feminist politics of community care – partial, patchy and reluctant perhaps, but nonetheless an indication that the feminist agenda has begun to make an impact on government policy? If so, do they open up the way for further demands to be pursued and for a significant re-shaping of community care policies to take account of the feminist critique and to develop along lines which do not rest upon the unpaid labour of women carers?

In this last section, I shall argue that these changes do indicate that feminism has made an impact on the community care agenda but that these inroads have been made by feminist demands of a particular type which can be characterized variously as 'equal rights', 'liberal' or 'reformist' feminism (Banks, 1981; Eisenstein, 1981; Dale and Foster, 1986). This is a tradition of feminism which has long historical roots, and which generated the initial feminist gains in relation to property law in the late nineteenth century, the vote (finally and fully in 1928) and the legislation in the 1970s concerning equal pay and sex discrimination. The demand that Invalid Care Allowance should be available to women on equal terms can be seen as one more successful battle related to the principle of equal rights. In order to assess both the strengths and the weaknesses of this particular feminist agenda in relation to community care, it is useful to look at the historical roots of this tradition and at the criticisms which can be made of it generally from other feminist positions.

What is equal rights, or liberal, feminism? The essence of this position is that it emphasizes the rights of individual women to be treated in the same way as individual men, and looks to the law to secure those rights. The emphasis is thus upon the removal of discrimination and of formal barriers to women's access to a position, organization, service or financial benefit. It is an emphasis which was present in the earliest feminist movement in Britain in the mid-nineteenth century, which produced the central focus for the successful struggle for women's access to professional occupations and to higher education and for the right to vote, and which even survived (especially in the trade union movement, with campaigns for equal pay) during the middle years of the twentieth century when feminist activity was much muted and reduced (Banks, 1981). The campaigns which finally produced the Equal Pay Act 1970 and the Sex Discrimination Act 1975 were not – as many people suppose – a consequence of the re-emergence of feminism in its new and more radical form in the late 1960s, but were in fact part of this historical pressure for the extension of equal rights for women. The continuity was not merely in terms of ideas, but also in the organizations which were campaigning for these measures. Women trade unionists had been pressing the equal pay case on the Labour Party since the end of the Second World War, and when Labour got back to power in 1964 it had a manifesto commitment to introduce this, which was not actually implemented for another six years (Banks, 1981). Other groups which had their origins in the first wave of feminism, notably the Fawcett Society and the Six Point Group, were prominent in pressure group activity at this time (Meehan, 1985).

This tradition of equal rights feminism has been the most significant in relation to mainstream politics and has underscored a series of legislative changes. Its strengths are clearest in relation to securing the position of individual women who are able to take advantage of the right to be treated in the same way as individual men. The emphasis is upon the removal of barriers to the equal treatment of women, and perhaps more subtly in changing the social and political climate so that unequal treatment becomes less acceptable. As Coote and Campbell (1982, p. 106) put it, in their comment upon the Sex Discrimination Act, this legislation probably helped slowly to change the climate of male–female relationships so that at the very least 'it ceased to be respectable to treat women less favourably than men – at least without making some effort to disguise what one was doing'. That slow change of climate was, in my view, one of the factors (but only one) which made it difficult in the end for the government to resist the argument that ICA should be extended to married women. Indeed, when the Jacqueline Drake case was going through the European Parliament and the government was in the final stages of trying to resist on ICA, it is notable that ministers did not attempt to deny the force of arguments about equality of treatment, but concentrated on arguing that they had the responsibility to consider how best to use any additional resources to support carers. As Tony Newton (then Social Services Minister) said in Parliament in February 1986:

> One problem is that if £85 million were available – that would be the cost [of extending ICA to married women] – it is far from clear that this would be the best way of giving additional support to those who are caring in the community . . . the best thing we can do for carers is to ensure that further services are available to them and that might be a better use of the resources involved. (House of Commons Official Report, vol. 92, 1985–6, Col. 803)

On one level, the impact of equal rights feminism is a considerable success story, yet many feminists would consider it something of a disappointment. This of course is partly because of various loopholes in the law which mean that women in practice do not have all the rights that they thought they were going to get. But more significantly from the perspective of my discussion here, it can be argued that the basic orientation of the equal rights agenda is too specific and too limited to make a real impact on the oppression of women.

Briefly, the arguments can be summarized as follows. First, the aims of the kind of change encouraged by the equal rights tradition by their nature benefit individuals, and some individuals – namely, as Banks puts it, 'the propertied and the educated' – are in a better position than others to take positive advantage of them (Banks, 1981, p. 243). Second, the liberal feminist position is reformist in the sense that it seeks limited and piecemeal changes within the structure of the existing society rather than a fundamental change in the way that society is organized, and may therefore only end up scratching the surface of the real causes of women's oppression. In so far as other feminist traditions see women's oppression built into the whole structure of the way in which society is organized (which applies in different ways to both radical and socialist feminists in Britain) the reformist position may simply look like a waste of time

(Dale and Foster, 1986, pp. 147–52). Third, whether or not one accepts this critique of the reformist position, it can be argued that the focus of equal rights feminism and the changes which it advocates are necessarily in the public sphere, where laws can be enforced, whereas these changes leave quite untouched the private sphere of family and marital relationships which lie at the root of women's oppression, and in particular do not challenge the traditional division of labour between women and men which lies at the heart of women's inability to be members of any society on equal terms with men (David and Land, 1983; Lewis, 1983).

Put together, these criticisms indicate that, from the position of other feminist perspectives, the liberal or equal rights tradition of feminism leads at best to very limited gains for women because the focus is on the individual rather than the collective interests of women. Most obviously, it is no good giving women individual rights to participate in the labour market if most of them are unable to take advantage of those rights because they are expected to do unpaid work in the home. In so far as the liberal feminist position avoids that issue it is not only limited in scope but also naïve, because it makes the implicit assumption that there is no fundamental conflict of interest between women and men. The radical feminist position in particular contrasts with that, because from this perspective it is clearly in men's interests to maintain the status quo, and it is assumed that men will not willingly give up the power and privilege which they now enjoy.

How does this discussion of the strengths and weaknesses of the liberal feminist position apply to the politics of community care? Clearly the pressure to extend benefits which support carers to women on the same terms as men is consistent with the classic equal rights agenda; but like the increased concern to 'support the carers' it does not represent any challenge to the traditional division of labour which ensures that many more women than men are actually doing caring work. Indeed, the experience of social policy change in Britain, and more broadly of political change, suggests that community care policies could go considerably further in incorporating the liberal feminist agenda, by making a range of benefits and services available to carers (both women and men on equal terms of course) without making any fundamental difference to the division of caring labour. Such changes would be very much in line with the assumptions about women which have been built into the structure of the British welfare state, namely that women are to be treated for all practical purposes as the dependents of men, and that the structures of state welfare should support their activities specifically as mothers, but also more generally as people who care for others, but not, for example, as workers (Wilson, 1977; David and Land, 1983). Whilst the character of the welfare state has changed over time in the ways I discussed earlier, this particular dimension has not, and we see it re-emerging in a new form in policies which aim to provide services which 'support the carers'.

At this point, the criticisms of the liberal feminist position become especially pertinent. Whilst it is certainly true that individual women's position as carers will be improved by changes of this kind, the idea of equal rights in caring provides a very clear illustration of how the liberal feminist agenda does not get to the heart of women's oppression because it does not touch on change in the family sphere (Lewis, 1983). Indeed, it can be argued that policy changes which make family care practically and financially more bearable for women can have the effect of actually strengthening the underlying traditional division of labour. The debate at this point becomes similar to the issue of 'wages for housework' which engaged the women's movement for some time in the 1970s, where the issue is whether the short-term gains for individual women in having their unpaid work socially recognized and supported would in effect undermine longer-term attempts to produce a society in which housework and caring are no longer seen as women's work. That is the same dilemma into which the liberal feminist agenda for community care leads us, and there is no easy solution to it.

## Developing the feminist agenda

My own position, as I have made clear elsewhere (Finch, 1984), is that it would be wrong not to continue to press for more support for women who currently do take on unpaid caring with little or no financial or practical support for the sake of potential longer-term gains. Like Eisenstein (1981), I would take the view that it is important for feminists who wish to secure more fundamental changes to work alongside liberal feminists, partly because some real gains for women can be achieved in that way. At the same time, the liberal feminist agenda for community care does in the end represent a very limited form of feminist demands and the task for feminists wishing to go beyond that is to formulate additional demands which do centrally seek for change in the division of labour between women and men in the private as well as the public sphere.

I make no claims to have worked out a coherent programme of this type, nor indeed would it be appropriate for me to do so: the spirit of feminism which is concerned with women's collective interest requires that women work out their demands collectively. But in broad terms it is possible to see the kind of issues upon which such demands would need to focus, and I shall sketch out briefly what I think they are, under two main headings.

First, there are matters concerned with social policy in general terms and across the whole spectrum of people's lives. At the very least, this is a matter of overcoming a situation in which equal opportunities policies in one area are undermined by policies in other areas which effectively make women's lives more confined. More positively, feminists who have thought about how social policy can support and encourage more radical changes in relationships between women and men have tended to look to the kind of measures introduced in some other European and Scandinavian countries, often under the general heading of 'family policy', which acknowledge the caring responsibilities of male and female workers by allowing periods of leave for routine child care, or a shorter working week for parents. For example David and Land (1983), in their discussion of how the goal of real equality between women and men might be achieved, argue that a range of social and economic policies would have to encourage a radically changed view of family relationships by such measures as a shorter working day. Another obvious and important set of measures would concern women's economic position, and a series of measures which feminists have sometimes referred to as the 'disaggregation' of incomes, which would ensure that each adult individual was treated as an independent economic unit, thus freeing women from economic dependency on men and – *inter alia* – making them less obviously available to perform unpaid caring tasks.

These kinds of measures would seem rather obviously necessary as 'background' changes to any serious attempt to remove unpaid women carers from their central role in community care policies. It is difficult to see how other measures in the field of community care specifically could succeed without these associated changes, but at the same time it would be unwise to assume that it would be easy to change the balance of power and the division of labour between women and men by these measures alone. Certainly, it is possible to argue that the example of Sweden, which probably represents the most progressive version of a coherent social policy strategy that seeks to create equality in the private as well as the public sphere, has shown that there are limits to the real changes which can be stimulated by these kinds of policies. Those limits can be seen at the point where it becomes obvious that further advances towards a non-sexist society can only be made if men start to give up some of their power (Scott, 1982). Such policies may not produce the ultimate changes which feminists seek, therefore, but they are probably an essential step in that direction.

Second, there are measures specific to the field of community care. Partly this is a matter of promoting different models for the care of dependent people, but it also entails changing the terms in which the debate about these issues is conducted. The most limited forms of concrete changes would entail the promotion of different forms of community care which encourage men to take on unpaid caring tasks in equal numbers to women, for example, by greatly increasing the financial support available to carers. I am in fact rather sceptical about whether it is ever going to be possible to make caring non-sexist in that sense, for reasons which I have set out elsewhere (Finch, 1984). But even if this were possible, it might not necessarily be a state of affairs which feminists would want to support, partly because it keeps caring for dependent people in the family domain as a privatized activity, and partly because one would want to defend the right of women who need care to be cared for by other women, not by men.

It seems to me that the more promising approach to developing a set of feminist demands about caring for dependent people is in fact to question whether the concept of 'community care' is appropriate at all. On the surface this would put feminists right out of line with almost all other current sectional interests (as I indicated earlier) but it would, in my view, be consistent with the way the feminist critique has already been developed. However, beneath that surface appearance of being out of line with the dominant consensus, I believe that there are ways in which a direct challenge to the orthodoxy of community care could be posed which would also have

resonance for other interests in the field. Such an over
serves to expose the confusions in present policy and pra
might conceivably form the basis of alliances with oth
groups to press for a re-evaluation of the whole comm   ᴊ ᴄᴀɪᴄ
emphasis in policy.

One such way in which the feminist challenge can be expressed is
the assertion that 'community care need not mean family care'.
Another way in which the same challenge could be posed is to say
that we want to replace care 'by' the community with care 'in' the
community. In other words, a set of feminist demands could be
formulated which would capitalize on the shifting meanings of
community care, and in effect would promote a version of it which is
somewhat more akin to the orthodoxy of the 1960s than the 1980s.
Policies devised on the basis of non-family care 'in' the community
would have to concern themselves with how to provide a range of
residential facilities, with nursing and domestic support attached,
which would enable elderly and handicapped people to lead as
independent and normal lives as possible, but in which the care
would be provided by people who are properly paid for doing so.
The de-emphasizing of family care as the central feature of
community care might well receive the support of handicapped
people themselves, for whom personal independence is a key goal.
Where is personal independence if one is obliged to rely on one's
family for support, through lack of alternatives (Finch, 1986)? Of
course within such settings attention would need to be paid to
enabling people to maintain links with people (relatives or friends)
to whom they are emotionally close, that is, people who care 'about'
them; but in my view, removing the compulsion to perform the
labour of caring 'for' one's relatives is likely to facilitate rather than
to obstruct that (see Finch, 1984; 1986 for further discussion).

These are the issues upon which, in my view, a more radical
feminist agenda for community care needs to concentrate. I am
aware that some feminists would certainly regard this position as
not radical enough, in that I am assuming that feminists will want to
press for progressive reforms within the structure of pluralist
democratic politics. Some would argue that this approach to
feminist politics will never succeed because men will never willingly
give up their power in favour of women. I respect that position but I
cannot wholeheartedly support it when I consider the many
thousands of women who are carrying the huge burden of unpaid

caring right now. To develop a feminist agenda which goes beyond the principle of equal rights but which can be used to press for changes in the foreseeable future seems to me both an urgent and a necessary task.

## Notes

1. This chapter was written before the publication of the Griffiths Report (1988) *Care in the Community*. The changes envisaged therein are significant, but do not alter fundamentally the analysis in this chapter.

## References

Audit Commission for Local Authorities in England and Wales (1986), *Making a Reality of Community Care* (London: HMSO)

Bailey, R. and Brake, M. (1975), *Radical Social Work* (London: Edward Arnold)

Banks, O. (1981), *Faces of Feminism* (Oxford: Martin Robertson)

Bayley, M. (1973), *Mental Handicap and Community Care* (London: Routledge and Kegan Paul)

Coote, A. and Campbell, B. (1982), *Sweet Freedom: The struggle for women's liberation* (London: Pan Books)

Dale, J. and Foster, P. (1986), *Feminists and State Welfare* (London: Routledge and Kegan Paul)

David, M. and Land, H. (1983), 'Sex and social policy', in H. Glennerster (ed.), *The Future of the Welfare State: Remaking social policy* (London: Heinemann)

Department of Health and Social Security (1981), *Growing Older*, Cmnd. 8173 (London: HMSO)

Department of Health and Social Security (1985), *Community Care, With Special Reference to Mentally Ill and Mentally Handicapped People*, Government Response to the Second Report from the Social Services Committee, 1984–5 Session, Cmnd. 9674 (London: HMSO)

Eisenstein, Z. (1981), *The Radical Future of Liberal Feminism* (New York: Longman)

Family Policy Studies Centre (FPSC) (1984), *An Ageing Population*, Fact Sheet no. 2 (London: FPSC)

Family Policy Studies Centre (FPSC) (1986), *Caring Costs: The social security implications*, Briefing Paper (London: FPSC)

Finch, J. (1984), 'Community care: developing non-sexist alternatives', *Critical Social Policy*, no. 9, pp. 6–18

Finch, J. (1986), 'Community care and the invisible welfare state', *Radical Community Medicine*, Summer, pp. 15–22

Finch, J. and Groves, D. (1980), 'Community care and the family: a case for equal opportunities?', *Journal of Social Policy*, vol. 9, no. 4, pp. 487–511

Gardiner, J. (1983), 'Women, recession and the Tories', in S. Hall and M. Jacques (eds.), *The Politics of Thatcherism* (London: Lawrence and Wishart)

Groves, D. and Finch, J. (1983), 'Natural selection: perspectives on entitlement to the Invalid Care Allowance', in J. Finch and D. Groves (eds.), *A Labour of Love: Women, work and caring* (London: Routledge and Kegan Paul)

Henwood, M. (1986), 'Community care: policy, practice, prognosis', in M. Brenton and C. Ungerson (eds.), *Yearbook of Social Policy in Britain 1986/7* (London: Routledge and Kegan Paul)

House of Commons (1985), *Community Care, With Special Reference to Adult Mentally Ill and Mentally Handicapped People*, Second Report from the Social Services Committee, Session 1984–5, vol. 1, HCP 13–I (London: HMSO)

Land, H. and Ward, S. (1986), *Women Won't Benefit: The impact of the Social Security Bill on Women's Rights* (London: National Council for Civil Liberties)

Lewis, J. (1983), 'Conceptualising equality for women', in J. Griffith (ed.), *Socialism in a Cold Climate* (London: Unwin Hyman)

Meehan, E. (1985), *Women's Rights at Work* (London: Macmillan)

Ministry of Housing and Local Government (1969), *People and Planning: Report of the Committee on Public Participation in Planning* (London: HMSO)

Nissel, M. and Bonnerjea, L. (1982), *Family Care of the Handicapped Elderly: Who pays?* (London: Policy Studies Institute)

Parker, G. (1985), *With Due Care and Attention: A review of research on informal care* (London: Family Policy Studies Centre)

*Report of the Committee on Local Authority and Allied Personal Social Services* (1968), The Seebohm Report, Cmnd. 3703 (London: HMSO)

*Report of the Royal Commission on Mental Illness and Mental Deficiency* (1957), Cmnd. 169 (London: HMSO)

Rimmer, L. (1983), 'The economics of work and caring', in J. Finch and D. Groves (eds.), *A Labour of Love: Women, work and caring* (London: Routledge and Kegan Paul)

Scott, H. (1982), *Sweden's 'Right to be Human': Sex-role equality – the goal and the reality* (New York: M. E. Sharpe, Inc.)

Szyszczak, E. (1987), 'The future of women's rights: the role of European Community Law' in M. Brenton and C. Ungerson (eds.), *Year Book of Social Policy 1986–7* (Harlow: Longman)

Townsend, P. (1962), *The Last Refuge* (London: Routledge and Kegan Paul)

Walker, A. (1982), 'The meaning and social division of community care', in A. Walker (ed.), *Community Care: The family, the state and social policy* (Oxford: Blackwell)

Walker, A. (1986), 'Community care: Fact and fiction' in A. Walker, P. Ekblom and N. Deakin, *The Debate About Community Care: Papers from a seminar on 'Community in Social Policy'* (London: Policy Studies Institute)

Willmott, P. (1984), *Community in Social Policy*, Discussion Paper no. 9 (London: Policy Studies Institute)

Wilson, E. (1977), *Women and the Welfare State* (London: Tavistock)

# CHAPTER 4

# BOUNDARIES BETWEEN FORMAL AND INFORMAL CARE-GIVING WORK

## HAZEL QURESHI

This paper commences with a discussion of the ideas underlying the distinction between formal and informal care, and continues with an investigation of the extent to which these concepts can be usefully employed to describe the actual practice of caring for elderly people in formal and informal contexts. The areas of critical interest are: first, the perception that to receive informal care is the preference of those who are cared for, and the associated belief that to attempt to 'formalize' such care by, for example, offering payment, would be radically to change its nature; second, drawing upon an understanding of informal care in operation, an examination of the extent to which certain kinds of formal care can take on informal aspects, and what the consequences of this might be.

## The worlds of formal and informal care

Abrams (1978) posed a sharp opposition between the worlds of formal and informal care. Far from there being a continuous spectrum of types of care, with statutory services at one end, family and neighbourly help at the other, and voluntary help in between, he argued that there should be seen to be a clear dividing line between the principles of organization of informal and formal care. The most salient difference is found in the criteria of eligibility for services: eligibility for informal care is conferred by virtue of social relationships between individuals (care for a mother, a daughter or a friend, for example), whereas formal care is delivered by agents of an organization, to individuals in defined categories of need (such as children at risk, or the disabled).

A second important difference is that, in the informal sector, forms of intervention and desirable outcomes are not well specified, as they are in formal service delivery. Of course, there are 'rules' operating in the world of informal care, and part of this paper will attempt to delineate and describe such rules in operation. Nonetheless such rules are not to be found in written form, and, although social sanctions may be imposed on those who do not comply, there are no formal procedures for obtaining redress if recipients are dissatisfied. Indeed, with specific reference to social benefits such as affection or approval the 'rules' of social exchange demand that such social rewards cannot be explicitly exchanged or bargained about lest this compromise their genuineness as expressions of true feeling (Blau, 1964). The disadvantages of formal services are those associated with bureaucratic organizations: inflexibility, inability to deal with atypical cases, slowness of response and usurpation of power over consumers by professionals. However, the superior resources and professional expertise of such organizations are often valued by consumers. Typically, within a formal organization there are rules decreeing equal treatment of equal cases, and professional workers are not expected to perform additional services for some clients only, according to their own personal preferences.

The personally directed nature of informal care provides the key to both its advantages and disadvantages in comparison with formal care. Since such care is specifically directed towards certain people, others with similar needs may receive no assistance. This has the consequence, suggested Abrams (1978, p. 3), that by the standards of the providers of formal care the world of informal care is 'something of a disaster' because it does not secure equal provision for all cases in particular categories of need, and the level of services received by particular individuals may thus fall short of, or exceed, desirable targets. However, Abrams argued that from the point of view of the recipients of assistance, care provided by the informal sector was qualitatively different from (and superior to) formal sector care. In a number of papers Abrams (1977, 1978) expounded the theme that because informal care is embedded in pre-existing social relationships, it has a different *meaning* (from formal care) to recipients. In brief, caring for someone in a practical way in the informal sector is seen as an expression of *caring about* them as an individual. A further reason for inferring a *prima facie* preference for informal care might be that although there may be no obvious difference in instrumental benefits received in a caring exchange – commodities such as meals, shopping, laundry and so on – it is likely that those who receive services will prefer to be supplied by those who will also supply social benefits such as warmth, affection and interest; and these latter social rewards have to be personally directed to be experienced as genuine.

Of course, too great a concentration on what recipients may feel should not lead us to neglect consideration of the costs to those providing help. Informal care, as will be demonstrated, involves unequal gender divisions in relation to costs, work and responsibilities. Elderly people are not unaware of the difficulties their relatives may suffer, and this may affect their preferences among sources of help, and level of satisfaction with help received. It has been suggested that, implicitly, there is a conflict of interest between women whose lives and opportunities are restricted by meeting others' needs for care-giving work, and those who are dependent on their services. Walker (1983) argues that, particularly in relation to elderly people, the real conflict of interest is between elderly people, their family carers and the state. Clearly the question of the differential quality of informal and formal care is an important consideration in relation to these arguments, because, if it is thought that practical assistance provided informally is not replaceable by formal help without an accompanying reduction in its value to the elderly person, then this suggests that there could be a conflict of interest between elderly people and informal carers.

If informal care is experienced as qualitatively different by recipients, then concern arises firstly that the formal sector cannot adequately substitute for the informal sector, should this be necessary, and secondly, that replacement of informal care with formally provided care would be undesirable because the quality of care would be thus diminished. Such concerns illustrate why the question of 'boundary crossing' is important, because it is implied that to 'formalize' informal care is undesirable and will have destructive results, and also that informal care cannot be provided through formal organizations. The expressed views of policy makers show that the arguments about the superiority of informal care are used to add a moral gloss to the Government's actions in restricting expenditure on statutory services, and in emphasizing a view of the informal sector of care as part of a reservoir of resources which not only can, but ought to, be 'increasingly' tapped instead:

> Not only is the family the most important means through which we show our care for others. It is also the place where each generation learns its responsibility towards the rest of society. . . . I think the statutory services can only play their part successfully if we do not expect them to do for us things that we could be doing for ourselves. (Thatcher, 1981)

> The primary sources of support and care for elderly people . . . spring from personal ties of kinship, friendship and neighbour-hood. . . . Care in the community must increasingly mean care by the community. (DHSS, 1981)

However, the strict division between formal and informal care has been questioned. For example, in criticism of Abrams' identification of their 'antithetical' principles of organization it has been argued that in practice these distinctions are blurred. Seyd, Tennant and Bayley (1983) point out that a voluntary visitor may become friendly with the person visited, to the extent that the formal origin of the relationship is forgotten and the activities of the visitor part of the informal sector. This does illustrate the need for a dynamic perspective to complement Abrams' essentially static theoretical distinction. Whilst voluntary organizations are undoubtedly part of the formal sector in terms of their objectives and principles of organization, this has most relevance for the consumer at the moment of the initial delivery of service. From then on a dynamic view must be taken, in order to understand the development of informal elements in the relationship between the two people specifically involved. This applies equally to statutory services: there is considerable evidence (Hunt, 1978; Sinclair *et al.*, 1984) that home-helps in many areas do develop personalized relationships with some clients, and this may include extra visiting and even taking the elderly person to the worker's own home. However, it is clear that these activities are undertaken by the worker's own choice, it is likely that the home-help behaves in this way only with selected clients: she personalizes her service to these few only, and thus, only by stepping outside her formal role as an agent of the state (in which all clients must be treated equally), can she offer genuine informal social rewards. If such effective benefits were coerced, or required as 'part of the job' then it seems they would lose much of their meaning to the participants in the relationship.

Even when services provided by the state are purely instrumental, there is some evidence that elderly recipients of state services see these as an expression of *caring about* them. For example, a study of elderly recipients of meals-on-wheels in Leeds (Johnson, 1981) concluded that the symbolic function – of demonstrating that people were cared about – was the main function being served by the service as it was then operated.

## Caring in practice

The next section will consider the results of two studies of people performing care-giving work, the first of which provides a detailed look at the informal sector of care in operation, thus establishing a context for the second study which focuses upon an attempt to generate community care for elderly people through formal means.

One focus of interest in each study was why those who helped were doing so, and the complex of reasons which influenced helpers in each study will be used to illustrate some of the particular characteristics of informal care, to compare this with care given initially on a formal basis, and to discuss what might be understood by transitions between these two types of care. As has been stated, one study was directly of the informal sector: the world of relatives, friends and neighbours providing assistance to people aged 75 or more living in Sheffield. The other was of formally provided care: a study of paid and, occasionally, unpaid helpers recruited to work on a Community Care Project financed by a social services department. In both instances those receiving care were elderly people; however, whilst the informal carers were assisting people with a wide range of difficulties, the clients of the Kent Community Care scheme were all sufficiently disabled to be considered to be on the margin of need for residential care. The Kent project social work team had a budget, and could spend up to two-thirds of the cost of residential care per week on each client. The team knew the costs of statutory services and were expected to put together cost-effective packages of care for individual clients within the budget constraints. Where a home-help was thought to be appropriate then this would be allocated and notionally included in the cost of the package. This meant that there was no possibility of home-help services being replaced by Kent project helpers in practice, although the principle of the scheme does not preclude this. (For a detailed discussion of the ideas behind the scheme and the Kent implementation see, for example, Challis and Davies, 1986.)

## Why do people say they help?

In both studies one area of inquiry was the question of why those giving assistance were doing so, but the reactions and answers to this question were strikingly different. The forty helpers on the Kent Community Care project were interviewed on two occasions: at an early stage to determine reasons for first offering their services, and again after up to a year of involvement to determine reasons for remaining involved (or leaving). To all Kent scheme helpers the question of why they were involved seemed a reasonable one, which they were prepared to consider at some length on each occasion. In contrast, the family helpers in Sheffield were sometimes taken aback, wondering what was meant by the question. Where explanations were offered they tended to be either simple statements of the family relationship ('I am her daughter' or 'there is no-one else', meaning no other family member), or, alternatively, explanations of why some other member of the family did not help ('her son's had two strokes so I go up and do it' [niece]). It seemed that there was an implicit set of expectations about who should provide routine assistance to elderly people, and that actions in conformity with these expectations were so obvious as not to require explanation. Only where the carer was 'unexpected', as in the case of the niece, was any explanation necessary.

Many studies have shown a preponderance of daughters among those giving help to elderly people, and the Sheffield study was certainly no exception: just over half (52 per cent) of all those elderly people receiving at least weekly practical help were receiving such help from a daughter, although only half of these daughters were helping alone. A variety of other female and male relatives (including spouses, sons and daughters-in-law) were engaged in providing assistance, and detailed analysis showed that this apparent diversity was the result of a systematic process of choice within the 134 informal networks considered. A hypothetical decision-rule based on an interaction between closeness of the kin relationship and ideas about appropriate gender roles, was able, in many cases, to predict who the principal helper or helpers might be. The detailed analysis and findings derived from the use of this model are contained in Qureshi and Walker (1989).

Qualitative evidence from those giving help supported the view that belief in such a hierarchy of obligation did affect people's feelings and actions. In particular, the view that the type of assistance required was 'women's work' was widely held. Where 'unexpected' people were helping, and had been interviewed, it was possible to examine their accounts of why the expected helper was *not* doing so. From these accounts it was possible to discover a number of 'acceptable' reasons for failure to discharge obligations. Where reasons were not considered acceptable, there were expressions of disapproval or accounts of conflict over what people should do. Acceptable reasons were personal ill health or incapacity, prior informal obligations to immediate family members, and unacceptable behaviour by the elderly person. This last was, naturally, susceptible to differing interpretations: reasons for family quarrels were not always evident, although there were a few instances in which children had disapproved of their parent's marriage after widowhood, or parents disapproved of children's divorce. There were some carers (mostly children) who provided assistance despite reporting considerable difficulties in their relationship with the elderly person in the past. Indeed, there was a minority (18 per cent) of those children who were helping who did not feel close to their parents and who reported neither past nor present help from them. Such children felt no personal sense of debt:

She's never been a Mother as Mothers should be, love . . . . She was out every day of her life and she didn't want anyone, any kids, any daughters' troubles, coming to her house to upset her routine.

I've been helping them since I was eight years old . . . . I remember going to the shop for my Mum, she's always been ill, every time we came home from school she was laid on the settee with a cold cloth to her head. Mum got five younger than me, well I brought them kids up. Every time I got home my Mum had got this, she said she had bilious bouts.

However, to resist the pressure to provide care had proved extremely difficult. This was not simply a matter of fear of what others might say (although this was present), nor of the influence of internalized value beliefs (which were also present). It was also the case that other people, formal and informal alike, *actively* demanded that relatives should provide care:

> Well she didn't ask, love. But I were forced to give it to her. Well, telephone went – it were next door neighbour – 'I've found your mother on the kitchen floor, she's fell, it looks like she's damaged her hip so' – 'Have you called the Doctor?' 'Yes, but could *you* come over' . . . from that day onwards . . . if anything's wrong they ring over here.

> The neighbours themselves don't want to know. Like down there, they didn't want to know my Dad, they wanted him moving, and yet they used to say, 'What's his daughter doing about it, she only lives up the bloody road', you know, this sort of thing, and this used to come back to me. It was told to me by various people.

Formal carers were no less likely to expect family care:

> Before Betty used to go over there regular she used to have it [home-help] twice a week . . . . One day the women of the social service . . . came up, found Betty there and said, 'I didn't know she had a daughter.' Oh yes – because she had a daughter she's [down to] four hours a week now.

> The people above [neighbours] fetched the police numerous times to him. The police used to come here and used to say 'What are you going to do about your father?'

However, it should be stressed that for most children, the external pressure to conform, exerted through the media (articles in the papers, or on TV) or through formal or informal contacts, were reinforced by their own personal sense of debt to the elderly person:

> Any time I needed her, well she'd come at the drop of a hat, so I feel I owe it back, you see, when she needs it. It works both ways, doesn't it? [Daughter]

> and they [parents] were always good to us so I think well we should be good to them, shouldn't we, they've looked after us. [Daughter]

A few helpers felt quite unequal to the task of repayment:

> As I say, she struggled to bring me up and that's it. It's always been there. It's always there. As I say, I never think I do enough. [Daughter]

As we have seen, such personalized commitment has been considered to underlie the alleged superiority of informal help. However, there are two points which should be made.

First, that to be a family member can be a unique disadvantage as well as, more usually, an advantage in dealing with a particular elderly person. The history of the relationship between an elderly person and their children is not always one of mutual exchanges of assistance and affection, and behaviour towards family members can be *worse* than behaviour towards others:

> I got to the point that I was trembling, and I couldn't sleep for thinking about it, but I used to start and walk down the road, and by the time I got to the corner I used to think 'it's my father and I have got to do it'. . . . As a child I was terrified of my father and I never ever lost this business of being afraid of him. . . . I'm his daughter and he feels he can hit me when he likes.

Other carers commented that their relative 'put on a different face' (usually a more co-operative face) when dealing with people outside the family, but felt entitled to take the services of their children for granted. Other research (Boyd and Woodman, 1978) has commented on the phenomenon of some elderly people displaying a degree of independence in a hospital or residential setting, but instantly losing this on being discharged home to the care of relatives. Instances in which elderly people were felt to have treated family members, in particular, in an uncaring way were a minority, of course, but as we have seen such relatives were always faced with the *prima facie* assumption by others that they were the best people to help.

The second point to be made is that elderly people did not always prefer informal help. One in ten of those receiving family assistance but no home-help, said that they would prefer home-help, and this was overwhelmingly because of a desire to relieve a perceived burden on the carer. Elderly people did not seem to feel that the performance of practical help was necessary in order to obtain social rewards, on the contrary, it seemed that sometimes the

obligation to provide too great a burden of instrumental assistance
could be positively damaging to social relationships. Although, in
general, deterioration in feelings was only reported by carers when
there were disputes about the legitimacy of demands made by the
elderly person.

> Now I do feel it's just a duty and it's not for the love of a parent, you
> know . . . for care. . . . After so long, I get really uptight inside
> because I don't care like I used to care and I think that causes, you
> know, it upsets me and I get depressed about that because I feel I
> should care, but I'm afraid I don't these days. . . . That upsets me
> more than anything, I think – I think that the feeling, you know, most
> of the feeling that I had for mother has vanished. [Daughter]

Taking account of the views of elderly people and their families, it
is clear that the assumption of a general preference for informal care
is too simple a view. Particular family members may be irreplace-
able in some ways – a visit from a voluntary visitor does not have the
same meaning as a visit from a daughter – but it is not easy to see
why this argument about social contact necessarily extends to the
performance of practical tasks. Equally there are within-family
differences, for example, personal care may be acceptable from a
spouse but not from children, who may not be preferred to formal
help. One elderly man accepted such help from his daughter-in-law
(rather than his daughter) because she was a nurse.

General attitudes, and policies, towards elderly people and their
families rest upon widely held stereotypes about the gender
appropriacy of particular tasks, especially routine domestic tasks,
and the debt owed by children to parents, as well as love and
affection within families. Even if this stereotype is true in most
cases, its application causes considerable suffering to those for
whom it is not true, and this group is, of course, likely to be
disproportionately represented among those who seek statutory
help. Families who wish to care should be helped but not all families
should be expected to care.

## Professionalizing the informal

What would constitute a transition from informal to formal help?
With regard especially to neighbours and relatives, the introduction

of payment in return for contractual regular commitment is one possibility. There seems to be little evidence about the effect of the introduction of payment into pre-existing informal relationships. Although there *have* been some schemes involving paid 'good neighbours', direct payments to relatives (on the lines of the pattern of home help service followed in some areas of Norway (Wærness, this volume)) have not been adopted in the UK. One of the Kent helpers interviewed had been giving some help to her elderly neighbour before she was recruited by the project and was asked to increase her involvement, in return for payment. In fact this particular arrangement soon broke down because it seemed that the elderly client viewed this change in the basis of the relationship as a transition to a totally new situation. The helper's husband commented: 'She thought she could have her just when she wanted her'; the elderly person seemed to feel free to call on her neighbour at any hour of the day or night, and had been known to knock on the wall at 11 p.m. and ask for her pillows to be straightened (a task which she had no difficulty in performing unaided).

However this cautionary tale cannot be taken as indicative of what a general trend might be. Only further results from other studies, where pre-existing helpers become paid, can develop a more general picture. The impression gained from the Sheffield study was that, within families at least, payment was not thought to change the character of the help given. When elderly people were asked whether they would prefer paid help (if they could afford it), to family help, a number replied that if they had sufficient money they would prefer to give it to their existing informal helpers. It was clear that this would not convert the caring exchange into an economic exchange of money for labour. In a formal economic exchange, the performance of the work would be conditional upon payment, whereas this clearly was not the case in the informal sector. To reinforce this view, it should be noted that about one in five elderly people did make gifts or loans of money to their children, and these were not conditional upon assistance from children, but rather depended on the relative resources of the generations (Qureshi and Simons, 1987).

Of course, the discriminating conditions governing the payment of benefits such as attendance allowance and invalid care allowance have meant that the 'complication' of payment has all too rarely been introduced into women's informal care-giving work. Such evidence as can be gleaned from the Kent study is minimal, because very few of the Kent helpers had any prior knowledge of the clients to whom they were allocated. Many clients of the scheme did not have locally available informal helpers. This partly reflects the location of the Project: a seaside town in South-East England (a popular retirement resort), but it may also reflect the fact that elderly people who did have an active network of local friends and relatives to provide help were probably less likely to be referred as being in need of residential care.

At the initial interview, it was clear that most Kent helpers subscribed strongly to the beliefs about family responsibility outlined in the discussion on family care:

> If my mother was ill I would give up everything to look after her. I just can't understand these people.

However, this level of identification with elderly people was not always maintained. Sometimes helpers, at second interview, in the light of their own experiences with the elderly person, had revised their opinion of relatives. Another helper commented:

> I haven't found her family irresponsible at all. At the beginning I used to wonder, but you have to get to know. No I don't blame her family at all. I think they've been martyrs . . . her children . . . they are very nice people and they've had such a life with her that they just tolerate her now . . . if this lady was my mother I would have abandoned her years ago. I really would. I wouldn't bother with her at all if she were my mother. That may be a dreadful thing to say, but that's how this lady is.

Of course, there were instances where the helpers could see no obvious reason for the failure of family members to help, and in such cases they continued to express disapproval. In other cases, good relationships were developed between helpers and family members, with the latter expressing gratitude to helpers for their assistance with relatives, and the former expressing pleasure at being able to relieve a burden on relatives.

## From the formal towards the informal: Kent Community Care helpers

Few helpers considered the project work to be a form of paid employment, and as such it was clearly unsatisfactory. Most helpers were women who, by virtue of age or family responsibilities were excluded from the labour market. The few men who helped were either young, unemployed and seeking experience for a job in the caring professions or (in one case) permanently disabled. Nonetheless, since, in general, helpers had no prior knowledge of their clients, their initial involvement was clearly on a formal basis: they offered their services to a project involving elderly people on the margin of need for residential care, without a specific client in mind, and were issued with a contract specifying tasks to be done and, in most cases, a rate of remuneration.

The clear formal basis made the initial meeting easier:

> Well I would say that it helps in the beginning. I mean you've got to go into a home and do a certain job to start with. You can't sort of walk in willy-nilly and say 'I'm here dear', you know, 'what can I do?' because people don't react the same way.

However, at second interview, helpers were inclined to deny the importance of the contract:

> Just a piece of paper.

> I don't know what it says now, I just filed it and put it away and that was that.

Those who could remember the contents of their contracts often denied that it truly reflected the level of their involvement:

> The contract doesn't show actually what you do, the hours you do . . . you know, the contract says an hour here and an hour there, but you can't keep to the contract.

A few helpers explicitly mentioned that they had developed a friendship with their clients, but this degree of attachment was rare. Many helpers said that they were 'friendly' towards their clients or 'attached to them' but stopped short of describing the relationship as one of true friendship. Therefore the helpers' later relationships cannot be described as informal. However, there were many

indications that some evolution away from the initial formal basis
had occurred. Four areas of change will be described.

First, helpers performed a number of tasks outside those
specified in the contract:

> I cooked. I did her dinner but it ended that I was doing her washing
> and everything else.

> I was only supposed to go and talk to her, but I was feeding her and
> doing other things.

> If I know that her neighbour is away on a Saturday morning and
> no-one is going to go in there all day I'll drop in there and just put her
> shoes on and sit and have a chat with her.

Second, helpers expressed an 'unprofessional' reluctance to
change clients, even, for example, when moving house had
increased the travelling distance considerably:

> My husband said to me, 'I think it's going to be a bit much for you
> going up and down, perhaps you could ask for someone a bit closer'.
> But I said to him 'it wouldn't be the same just swapping and changing
> because you get used to the person as much as anything'. I think you
> do tend to get attached to the actual people you're visiting.

This attachment to clients did sometimes extend to the assumption
of some degree of personal responsibility for their welfare, a sense
that the helper was not easily replaceable as an individual in the life
of the client:

> Well, you can't leave them. You can't go to them and then stop. You
> know you can't don't you? Once they get used to you, you
> can't. . . . I said I realize I've got them until they do die.

Indeed, half of the helpers questioned considered, at second
interview, that the main factor sustaining their involvement was
their client's dependence on them. Some helpers with children
explicitly equated the two types of responsibilities.

> They do depend on us and I couldn't let them down. They're like the
> children. I just couldn't let the children down so I certainly can't let
> them down.

Finally, those helpers with families tended to involve them in
looking after the elderly person. About one-third of helpers

mentioned some involvement of this kind. Some husbands helped with practical tasks such as hedge-cutting, and carpet laying. Sometimes other members of the helper's family were sent along to the elderly person instead of the helper:

> If something came up and I couldn't go, then the boy, my eldest boy, would go and do the same jobs under supervision of the lady.

One in five helpers reported that clients had come to visit them in their own homes:

> If you develop a relationship with somebody, and you know they are depressed at weekends and can't manage – you have them over here.

> She'll sit in there while I get the dinner and she'll help me wipe up and clear away. She can eat it, she can drink and smoke – other people you don't bring out. They don't leave their homes, so it's a different type of client.

In which instances was such additional involvement unlikely to manifest itself?

> It's very difficult if you have an incontinent person. You see, you can't have them in your homes. I know it sounds awful but there are not many people that would have people that are incontinent in their homes, and I don't feel I can.

> I wouldn't let them [become involved]. I wouldn't let them because of the way that she is. If she'd been a different type of person I probably would have done . . . but she tends to grab hold of anybody, you know . . . when I said this morning that I was seeing you . . . all she wanted to know was whether she could claim anything from you, whether you did food parcels.

Four areas of change in relationship have been identified, which it is claimed indicate a change, over time, towards a more informal type of caring.

As has been illustrated, such developments did not occur with all clients, indeed it was clear that they would not always have been welcomed:

> Some people want you to get closer to them than others. Some people keep you just where you're meant to be, sort of thing . . . you know . . . if you're going there to help you just do what they want doing and you go. Sometimes there's barely a few words spoken.

However, most helpers interviewed gave accounts of the development of a relationship of some degree of warmth and affection with at least one of their clients, and frequently they referred to this possibility as being at the basis of the project work:

> I think this is part of the project whereby you do become friends with them rather than just a stranger popping in to make a cup of tea, you know.

> I think the project is . . . half of it is not what you do, it's your presence.

In a number of cases, helpers were quite clear that the relationship was so well established that they would carry on visiting independently from the project:

> Even, say [the social worker] said there was no need to go and visit Mrs Leggatt any more, I would still go, even though I wouldn't be paid for it, because she looks forward to seeing me and, she always says 'my friend Joan' you know, and she really is.

However, although in some cases helpers were prepared to maintain friendly contact without pay, some had a clear conception that they were unlikely to continue to provide more instrumental services, especially on a regular basis:

> I wouldn't give up visiting the ones that I know. I'd still go and see them. Of course, I wouldn't be able to bring them dinners, but I'd still go and spend half an hour with them, that type of thing.

Thus, a relationship which may have been established upon the basis of paid performance of practical tasks, may persist and survive even the cessation of payment. However, as illustrated by the helper above, a separation can be made between those expressive, supportive aspects of the relationship, from which mutual pleasure is derived, and the more instrumental, practical elements of caring for which it is expected that material return will be made. Implicit in the above helper's comment is a sense of freedom in relation to the performance of practical tasks, which is unlike that experienced by family helpers. Because the carer perceives the project social work team as responsible for the overall package of care for the elderly person, she is not 'trapped' into giving practical care by a perception that there is no alternative apart from her own care.

As one helper put it:

> It's not like a parent where you couldn't give them up. You see with family you are duty bound really . . . but with this you are not.

Another helper reported her resistance to the suggestion by the elderly person that the care she gave should no longer be channelled through the formal agency:

> My old lady suggested that I just came out of community care and took her on full-time, which was not a possibility because I knew I'd practically live in the house. I spend a lot of time there as it is, but I was not prepared to be committed to a full-time situation where she could say 'do this, do that', you know.

Ideally, the helpers saw the project social work team as their protection from being overwhelmed by the needs or demands of their clients. The ready access to the resources and expertise of the formal agency could prevent them from being pushed by a sense of obligation or guilt into giving more than they wished to give: in other words, could protect them from some of the undesirable features of informal care-giving, whilst enabling them to have the time and freedom to develop a personal relationship with a particular elderly person or people.

Unfortunately the ideal was not always realized. The changing relationship with elderly people meant that some helpers now came to feel that they had entered a kind of 'no-man's land' in relation to their work with elderly clients. If their activity was not to be viewed as an economic exchange, perhaps it was inappropriate to ask for more money as their level of activity increased (after all, they had not been 'officially' asked to do more). Equally, if inflation had eroded the value of the payments initially agreed, ought they to ask for payment to be raised? A number of helpers expressed ambivalence and confusion, and a few outright dissatisfaction over levels of payment. Such feelings were expressed by only about one in ten helpers, but they were people who had a high level of involvement, and their payments could have been raised. Later, regular review of payments was instituted, as it became clear that many helpers (although not all) were reluctant to raise this issue themselves.

The fact that helpers were paid for practical help, or for time spent giving emotional support, in no way militated against the development of a warm and friendly relationship over time, although this occurred only with selected clients, usually those who had something to offer in return. The views of clients (reported in Qureshi, 1985) suggested that, although elderly people did wish for their helpers to be paid, they sometimes indicated that they did not wish helpers to come because of the money. In other words, they too considered that there should be a material return for practical help, but, to be convinced that warmth and affection were genuine, had to be sure that these social benefits were not being bought.

## Principles of the Kent Community Care project

In the geographical area covered by the project, the level and intensity of statutory assistance to elderly people in the form, for example, of home-helps, community nursing and incontinent laundry services, was low. Thus, since the social workers began from an assessment of the needs of individual clients, helpers were often recruited to perform practical tasks, which in other areas might already be carried out by statutory services. In areas with a higher level of basic services, there might be more concentration on the relationship-building aspect of the helper's task, with helpers recruited for practical tasks only when the specific circumstances or characteristics of clients required it. In principle, at least, social workers need not use the strategy of recruiting helpers at all; they could choose to spend their budget in other ways. However, all replications have used this method of working.

Since, in contrast to informal carers, Kent helpers need not have chosen to join the project, it may be argued that any costs to them, involved in their participation, can be discounted in the overall assessment of cost-effectiveness. However, the dynamic perspective which has been adopted in this paper shows that, as commitment becomes more personally directed, it is possible for helpers to become trapped into continuing to provide care for an individual even though they may no longer feel that they are receiving sufficient returns. In this sense, any schemes which encourage individuals to enter into caring arrangements in which it is expected that informal elements may develop, contain not only the potential to achieve considerable improvements in the welfare of elderly people and informal supporters, but also for serious exploitation of individual workers. It need not be necessary to achieve the former at the expense of the latter; however, too great an emphasis on 'cost-effectiveness' without an accompanying explicit commitment towards a non-exploitative approach does carry this danger.

## Conclusion

Formal and informal carers are generally assumed to have in common the aim of improving the welfare of individuals. Although Abrams' theoretical distinction between the principles of organization of the worlds of formal and informal care is accepted, it has been argued that a dynamic view, of the process of development of relationships between individuals, can illustrate that transitions between these worlds are possible, and need not be destructive. Although there is little conclusive evidence, money for work does not appear to corrupt pre-existing informal relationships (especially if these are well established). Equally, informal, or quasi-informal, relationships can be generated from a formal basis, although such helpers have no wish to take on all the responsibilities of informal care, indeed the understanding that they will not have to do so underlies their commitment to continuing helping activity.

Investigation of the informal sector of care in Sheffield demonstrated clearly the widespread existence and persistence of informally provided care, in particular care by kin. The unwritten rules of kinship obligation, and ideas about gender roles, continue to exert a strong influence on behaviour, to the extent that even relatives who feel no sense of individual debt may be coerced into bearing the costs of care. Where assistance was not provided by relatives, even though relatives existed, there seemed to be little opportunity of generating it at a low cost. Either it was unlikely ever to be available, because of the potential carers' incapacity or antipathy towards the elderly person, or it could only be secured by incurring other costs (by providing forms of family therapy, or resources to relieve the carer of other informal obligations).

Since so many relatives do help, there is clearly an important role for statutory services in supporting those who do wish to assist their elderly relatives and friends. However, attention does have to be given to the question of what can be done to generate care which gives other elderly people the services they require. Given the prevalence of loneliness, depression and boredom among substantial minorities of elderly people (see, for example, Hanley and Baikie, 1984; Wenger, 1984), especially those who suffer from ill-health and disability, the task of relationship-building is one which should be attempted. The Kent experience demonstrates that the paid performance of practical tasks can be a basis for this, although an exclusive focus on the cost-effectiveness of the practical help provided, reduces the role of helpers to that of a supplement to inadequate formal help instead of an essential complement to it.

# References

Abrams, P. (1977), 'Community Care', *Policy and Politics*, 6, 2, pp. 125–51

Abrams, P. (1978), *Neighbourhood Care and Social Policy* (Berkhamsted: Volunteer Centre)

Blau, P. (1964), *Exchange and Power in Social Life* (New York: John Wiley)

Boyd, R. V. and Woodman, J. A. (1978), 'The Jekyll and Hyde Syndrome: an example of disturbed relations affecting the elderly', *The Lancet*, no. 8091, September 23, pp. 671–2

Challis, D. and Davies, B. (1986), *Case Management in Community Care* (Aldershot: Gower)

DHSS (1981) *Growing Older*, Cmnd. 8173 (London: HMSO)

Finch, J. and Groves, D. (1983), *A Labour of Love: Women, work and caring* (London: Routledge and Kegan Paul)

Hanley, I. and Baikie, E. (1984), *Understanding and Treating Depression in the Elderly*, in Hanley and Hodge, 1984, *op. cit.*

Hanley, I. and Hodge, J. (1984), *Psychological Approaches to the Care of the Elderly* (Kent: Croom Helm)

Hunt, A. (1978), *The Elderly at Home* (London: HMSO)

Johnson, M. (1981), Unpublished paper given at the International Congress of Gerontology, Hamburg

Qureshi, H. (1985), 'Exchange theory and helpers on the Kent Community Care Project', in *Research, Policy and Planning*, vol. 3, no. 1, pp. 1–9

Qureshi, H. and Simons, K. (1987), 'Resources within families: caring for elderly people', in Brannen J. and Wilson G. (eds.), *Give and Take in Families* (London: Allen and Unwin)

Qureshi, H. and Walker, A. (1989), *The Caring Relationship: Elderly people and their families* (London: Macmillan)

Seyd, R., Tennant, A. and Bayley, M. (1983), *The Home Help Service*, Paper no. 6, Dinnington Neighbourhood Services Project, Department of Sociological Studies, University of Sheffield

Sinclair, I., Crosbie, D., O'Connor, P., Stanforth, L. and Vickery, A. (1984), *Networks Project: A study of informal care, services and social work for elderly clients living alone*, National Institute for Social Work, Research Unit

Thatcher, M. (1981), *Speech to WRVS National Conference*

Walker, A. (1983), 'Care for elderly people: a conflict between women and the state', in Finch and Groves (eds.), 1983, *op. cit.*

Wenger, C. G. (1984), *The Supportive Network: Coping with old age*, National Institute, Social Services Library no. 46 (London: Allen & Unwin)

# CHAPTER 5

# WOMEN AND THE WELFARE STATE: BETWEEN PRIVATE AND PUBLIC DEPENDENCE

## A comparative approach to care work in Denmark and Britain

BIRTE SIIM

The radical changes in women's position in society during the last twenty years have been followed by a dramatic growth in feminist scholarship and in studies of women's position in society. In the first phase of feminist scholarship the focus has been on the study of the general oppression of women in society often related to structural contradictions within the two dominating systems of capitalism and of patriarchy.[1] Today there is a growing realization of the need for more comprehensive comparative studies that focus on the differences in women's situation in different societies and also within different classes, ethnic groups and cultures.[2]

The purpose of this paper[3] is to analyse how women's position in Denmark and Britain can be related to differences in the organization of social reproduction in the modern 'welfare state'. The paper will focus on the institutional differences in the organization of social reproduction of individuals and households in relation to care for children, the sick, the old and the disabled. The institutional differences between Denmark and Britain have long historical roots and are both an expression of differences in class structures and of differences in the political cultures of the two countries. I argue that the differences in the organization of social reproduction in Denmark and Britain, as they have developed during the last twenty years, have had important consequences for the position of women in society. In the article I look especially at the relationship between women's position as workers and mothers, and their activities as citizens.

In Denmark the welfare state project has brought with it a new partnership between the state and the family (and between women and the state). An important part of this new partnership was a growing state responsibility in relation to care for children, the old, the sick and the disabled during the 1960s and 1970s. This development has had important consequences for women, and has been one of the preconditions for the integration of women into the public sphere of work as a permanent part of the work-force. As a result women have increasingly become able to support themselves, and there has been a decrease in women's economic dependence on their individual husbands. Contrary to all expectations this development has not meant the abolition of the sexual division of labour and the end of male domination. What has happened can be interpreted as a change in the form of oppression, in the sense that women have become subjected to a new form of male domination in the public sphere. The expansion of the 'social' state has made women increasingly dependent on the state as public sector workers and as mothers and consumers of social services and to some degree as clients in the welfare system.[4]

The development of the modern welfare state in Britain has, in contrast, largely maintained a 'familist' organization of social reproduction as an integrated part of the system of social reform first advocated by the Beveridge Report, supported by the Labour Party, and continued into a newly revived 'familial' faith by the present Conservative government.[5] One effect of this familism has been that women were conceived primarily as mothers, which meant giving married women the main responsibility for care work. This has made women's integration into the public sphere of work very difficult, and women have largely therefore remained marginal workers. As a consequence married women have to a large extent remained economically dependent on their individual husbands and have only to a smaller degree been able to support themselves through wage-work. Women have become dependent on the state both as workers and mothers, but the family social policies have increasingly made women dependent on the state as clients as well.

The second part of the paper looks at how the questions of social welfare are related to questions of political power by focusing on women's political activities as citizens. I look at feminist strategies towards the welfare state and discuss women's role in the contemporary struggles about the future direction of the welfare states. I argue that differences in women's political activities as citizens in Denmark and Britain can be related to differences in women's position as workers and mothers. In the last part I discuss some of the theoretical and political challenges in analysing the welfare state from a feminist perspective.

## The welfare state and the different organization of social reproduction

In my studies of women and the welfare state I have found that it is important to be aware of the qualitative differences between the different forms of welfare states.[6] The Scandinavian principles of social welfare are in important ways different from other principles of social welfare. It is, nevertheless, problematic to put too much emphasis on defining a specific Scandinavian 'welfare model'. First of all there are important differences both between the ideas and the political practices of the Scandinavian countries. Secondly, a feminist perspective challenges the dominant theoretical framework behind the notion of a specific Scandinavian form. This framework is built primarily on the relationship between the state and the market economy and subsequently undervalues the relationship between the public sphere and the family. It is also important to emphasize that none of the Scandinavian countries represents an ideal 'model' from a women's point of view, because there still exists a sexual division of labour and a new form of male dominance in Denmark, Sweden and Norway. From a feminist perspective it becomes crucial to develop a theoretical framework that acknowledges the qualitative differences in the political cultures and in state institutions of the welfare state in relation to the public–private split and to the organization of social reproduction of individuals and households.

The Scandinavian principles of welfare are different from principles elsewhere, primarily because the right to the greater part of the social benefits is not conditioned by insurance nor by individual payments but is part of the individual's right as a citizen. The system is mainly financed by the tax system, and the administration of the system is in most cases carried out by the state or by the local state. Another important characteristic is connected with the character of the social services, which to a great extent are provided directly by the public service sector. These public services are predominantly available as free public goods, or at prices that are much lower than the economic costs (Esping-Andersen, 1981; Therborn, 1986).

These principles have nowhere been fully applied. (Unemployment insurance for example has been an exception to the principle in all the Scandinavian countries.) Compared to the other existing principles of social welfare there is, however, no doubt that the Scandinavian system is built on the most universal principles of solidarity with the groups outside the labour market and with the disadvantaged groups in general. This is the basis for the argument that the Scandinavian welfare states have been the most advanced also in relation to women (Ruggie, 1984). I will show that there is some truth in this argument, although it needs significant qualifications. There is an important difference between questions of social welfare and questions of political and economic power. One of the main points in this article is that there is no automatic relation between advances in terms of social welfare and advances in terms of political power. One important question is in what ways and to what extent the Scandinavian principles of social welfare have empowered women as mothers, workers and citizens.[7]

## The growth of the modern welfare state from a gender perspective

The welfare states have long historical roots, and during the last hundred years there has been a gradual development of state involvement in the economy and in relation to human reproduction. This has been described as a quantitative growth in both public and social expenditures as part of the Gross National Product (GNP), and as a quantitative growth in the number of public employees, especially within the social 'health' and educational sectors. It has been argued that it was not till the 1960s and the 1970s that the real social transformation of the modern welfare state appeared, in the sense of states in which expenditure on welfare state activities such as income maintenance, care and education became predominant.[8] In the following discussion, I focus on the more qualitative aspects of this social transformation of the Danish and the British welfare states in relation to social reproduction of individuals and households by giving a brief overview of the different types of organization of care work from a woman's perspective. How can the differences in the organization of care work be explained, and what is the impact of these differences for women?

## The new partnership between the state and the family in Denmark

In Denmark a new form of partnership between the state and the family has gradually developed since the Second World War. One of the cornerstones has been the acceptance of some kind of state responsibility for the organization and financing of care for children, the old, the sick and the disabled. These new ideas about the relationship between the public sphere and the private sphere of the family, and about the role of women in society, developed partly in response to socio-economic changes, and did not become part of official public policies till the 1960s and 1970s. From the point of view of women the most important thing was the acceptance and gradual institutionalization of women's dual roles as workers and mothers, and a political consensus about building a support system of social services and benefits to help women cope with this dual role.

The new partnership between state and the family in relation to care work developed under the influence and inspiration of the Social Democratic Party, which since the 1930s has been the leading political force behind the building of the Danish welfare state. The Social Democratic Party has been in government since the end of the 1920s, although always in a minority position dependent on alliances with other political parties. In Denmark, like Sweden, it has therefore been the Social Democratic version of the welfare state that since the 1930s has become the accepted political form of social welfare.

In the 1960s public responsibilities were extended to new areas of society – both in relation to the economy and in relation to social reproduction – and the notion of social citizenship became central to the new understanding of the welfare state. The general meaning of social citizenship was to secure the universal rights of the individual *vis-à-vis* the state:

> the right to a modicum of economic welfare security regardless of the position in the labour market and the right to share to the full of the social heritage and to live the life of a civilized being according to the living standards prevailing in society. (Marshall, 1983)

This right as a citizen, originally formulated by Marshall, became a working-class ideal about equality, but it was nowhere automatically extended to women. It is remarkable that the Social Democratic Party in Denmark developed an understanding of social citizenship that accepted motherhood and care work as part of the social responsibilities of the state, and subsequently built a network of institutions to support these ideas.

## Family policy as gender policy

After 1960 both the conception of the family and the principles and practice of social and family policy changed radically. During the 1930s Denmark had adopted a family policy, directed primarily towards poor families with children and towards single mothers. The purpose was to support the working-class family and create a greater equality for children from different classes through a publicly financed support system. The principle of right was introduced in the social legislation during the 1930s substituting the principle of evaluation of individual cases. After the Second World War this principle of individual rights was, however, developed further and extended to new areas of social policy. The new 'family' policy of the 1960s was no longer directed primarily towards the working-class and the poor, but towards all families, and it rested to a great extent on a system of public services. This new partnership between the family and the state was advocated by the Social Democratic Party, and it can be interpreted as a new kind of relationship between the private sphere of the family and the public sphere of the state, where care work has become in part the responsibility of the state and has thus become an accepted part of social citizenship.

The new organization of social reproduction of individuals and households touched upon many different areas of social policy. Some of the important areas from a women's viewpoint were as follows:

1. A system of family allowances to all children and a supplementary allowance to single parents, and a youth allowance which later became means-tested.
2. A housing policy that gave rent subsidies to families with low incomes and to single parents, through a non-profit housing association that owns about half of all rental houses.
3. Local responsibility for the building of public day care institutions according to social needs. The state pays about 80 per cent of the costs of having children in institutions, and the remainder is paid by the parents. About a quarter of all consumers pay either reduced rates or use the institutions free of charge.
4. A system of free health services and of free educational services from the primary school to the university level.
5. Local responsibility for the building of nursing and old age homes according to social needs.

## The new social organization of care

The development of this new organization of social care in Denmark was a gradual process. The principle of universal rights was clearly expressed in the new policies towards old age and child care that became part of social legislation in the late 1950s and early 1960s. The new reform of the Old Age Insurance system from 1956 gave all people over the age of 65 the right to an old age pension regardless of their previous and immediate income. And in 1964 a new law about care for old people was passed giving the municipal authorities the responsibility for securing an adequate number of places in nursing and old age homes, according to local needs. During the same year there were similar far-reaching changes in the purpose, form and substance of child care policies. Child care institutions now became directed towards and open for all children instead of only for the needy, and new educational and pedagogical principles like play and social interaction were given a very high priority. Child care, like care for the old, became part of the responsibility of the local state. There was a broad political consensus both about the general principles and about the specific pieces of legislation in both of these policy areas. In some areas there was, however, a political conflict over the extent of institutionalized social care.[9]

One consequence of the radical changes in the policies of social care was a dramatic rise in the 1960s and 1970s in both social expenditures and in social employment, i.e., employment in health care, education, day care and social work. In 1960 public expenditure was only 26 per cent of the Gross National Product, but by 1981 it had risen to more than 60 per cent, and the growth was strongest within the areas of education, health and care for children and the old. It is interesting that it is in the two areas of care for the old and care for children that the highest relative growth can be found. This development is no doubt connected to fundamental socio-economic transformations, such as the changing role of the family in society, and the integration of married women into the labour market. In Denmark the number of 'housewives' has fallen drastically during the last twenty years from 829,000 in 1960 to 250,000 in 1981, and the activity rates of married women have risen accordingly from 23 per cent in 1960 to 64 per cent in 1984, and are now approaching the participation rate of men, which was 78 per cent in 1984. In 1983 more than 70 per cent of women workers were employed in paid 'care work', i.e., in day care institutions, in homes for the elderly, and in health and educational institutions (Bent Rold Andersen, 1984, 1983a and b).

Research material from the Danish National Institute of Social Research can illustrate some of the effects of the changes on the lives of old people (Olesen *et al.*, 1976; Olesen, 1981). In 1964 the law gave the local state the responsibility to secure the necessary places in nursing and old people's homes. Between 1962 and 1977 the number of old people living with their children fell significantly. The number of single men over 80 living with their children (or relatives) fell from 41 per cent to 22 per cent, while the number of single women of the same age fell from 27 per cent to only 11 per cent during the same period. The reports also found a downward trend in the extent of daily contact between elderly persons and their children during the same period. In fact, the relative number of places in old people's homes and in nursing homes grew only slowly between 1965 and 1979. In 1979 the majority of old people in all age groups were still living in their own homes, rather than in institutions or with their family. However, there has been a dramatic growth in the cost of social care services provided for old people living in their own homes, e.g. home-help, home nursing, care work and housing support. This is an expression of a change in the policies of the local state towards old people during the 1970s where the provision of social services to old people in their own homes has been given a higher priority (Olesen, 1981).

During the same period the state has gradually taken over a larger responsibility for the care of children in public day care and child care institutions. Since 1965, and especially during the 1970s, there has been a dramatic growth in the relative number of places in public day care and child care institutions both for 0–2 year olds and for 3–6 year olds. By 1984 42 per cent of the 0–2 year olds and 57 per cent of the 3–6 year olds were enrolled full time in public day care and child care institutions. As a consequence, Denmark in 1984, together with Sweden, had the highest coverage of public day care and child care institutions in the western world.[10] The institutions that were largely built in the 1970s have relatively high standards, but there has been a deterioration of standards with the economic crisis, for instance, the number of children per teacher has risen. The economic stagnation has also meant that the parents' contributions have been gradually increased, although they still only cover about one-third of total costs.

## Women's dependency on the state as workers, consumers and clients

The breakdown of the earlier breadwinner–homemaker family has reduced the role of the husband as an economic provider for married women. Today women have become integrated as part of the permanent work-force, and by 1985 unskilled women earned more than 90 per cent of the average wage of unskilled men. The changes in family patterns and the growth of the dual-earner family have, however, not given men and women equal opportunities to provide for themselves and their children. Women have today to a greater extent come to rely on their own wage-work for economic survival and to a smaller extent on their husband's wages, but women's responsibilities as mothers and their unequal position in the labour market have increasingly made them dependent on the state, both as workers in the public service sector, as consumers of social services, and as clients in the social welfare system. Women's growing integration in the labour market has not created greater equality between male and female workers, and during the 1970s there has actually been an exacerbation of the sexual division of labour. It has therefore become increasingly important to discuss both women's relationship to the state and the principles of social policy.[11]

Women's growing dependency on the state is most sharply illustrated by the situation of the group of single mothers, who have come to rely heavily on the state for economic support both in terms of cash benefits and services. During the 1970s it became widely accepted that women often chose not to marry in the first place, or later decided that they wanted to live alone with their children. Unfortunately, during the same period it became increasingly difficult to provide for a family with only one income, because the social norm has today become a two-earner family. Single mothers have very high activity rates compared to such women in other welfare states. Thus in 1978 more than 80 per cent of single mothers with one child were in the labour force. This, on the one hand, is an expression of the fact that they have only their own earnings to support themselves, but on the other hand it is also an indication of their strong reliance on public services and support, especially in relation to child care. For this group the nature of state support in terms of how much and what kind of support they can expect becomes crucial for the social and economic well-being of themselves and their children. In Denmark, single parents have received rather generous support from the state, compared to most countries. State support in terms of public services and benefits forms an important part of their total income. They receive a supplement to the universal family allowance, which has today become means-tested, and they are eligible for special housing benefits and for economic subsidy for child care institutions.

The limitations of state policies in obtaining equality between women and men have become more visible with the economic crisis and the growth of mass unemployment since 1974. In Denmark there have not been any explicit attempts to push women out of the labour market, but many fear that the cut-backs in public expenditures together with the introduction of new technology in the future will marginalize many women in relation to the labour market, especially in the public and private service sectors. The whole institutional structure of the Danish welfare state has, however, come under pressure during the economic crisis, and the Liberal–Conservative Government that came to power in the election of 1981, especially, has clearly expressed the intention of giving market forces a greater importance in social policies.

## The familist organization of social reproduction in Britain

In Britain after the Second World War there developed a dual system of welfare: a state-administered system of social assistance directed at the poor and financed out of general taxation, and an insurance system based on benefits provided as of right. The 'familist' organization of human reproduction has been maintained in the sense that:

(a) the family still plays the most important role in the reproduction process, although the welfare state in different ways has modified and partially supplemented the family; and that

(b) the state has supported a family with a traditional sexual division of labour between the male breadwinner and a dependent wife.

This familist organization of reproduction dates back to the ideas of Beveridge. The Beveridge Plan was envisaged as a grand reform project to replace the prevailing poor laws, and it was put forward as a result of strong demands from the Labour Movement. The cornerstone of the reform was the establishment of a National Health Service (NHS) built on the universal principle of rights. One of the main principles of the new welfare system was insurance against old age, sickness, unemployment, invalidity, etc., which was supposed in general to give a minimum income to all who were in need. This social insurance principle covered all working people, and the right to benefits was as a rule conditional on a record of individual payments. A system of National Assistance (later Supplementary Benefits and now Income Support) was set up to cover exceptional cases of social needs. Another main principle was that the family was regarded as a single economic entity, with the husband as the breadwinner and the wife as dependant. In this way the family was given a fundamental role in social reproduction, and family policies and social policies hereafter became inextricably linked.[12]

Feminist researchers have analysed the assumptions, values and contradictions built into the British social policies and their impact on married women. First of all, the social security system embodies assumptions about women's economic dependency. Married women are supposed to rely on their husbands for financial support, which places strict limitations on a married or cohabiting woman's right to claim benefit in her own right. In the case of the husband's unemployment the extra dependency benefit is lost if a wife earns more than eight pounds a week; income support is likewise reduced pound by pound. This has given the wife a strong incentive to give up paid work once her husband becomes unemployed, unless her earnings are high enough to support the whole family. Secondly, the assumption behind the social security system is the notion that married women have the responsibility to care for their husband, their children and sick and elderly relatives, and until very recently married women were excluded from certain benefits on this ground. So even though the majority of married women today have paid work, they are still in the social legislation treated as though they were dependent upon their husbands.

This discriminatory social policy has very serious effects on women's social and economic position. The state, in contrast to Denmark, has not, to any large extent, taken responsibility for caring for children or the elderly. The general picture in relation to care for the elderly is that the majority of the elderly live in their own homes or with their children, and only a small minority (less than 2 per cent in 1975) live in residential institutions provided either by voluntary organizations or local authorities. The responsibility for care for the children is likewise predominantly a responsibility of the mother, in spite of married women's growing economic participation. In Britain there is still a dual system of care with a strong division between education and care for the under-fives. Care for the under-fives is not, like education, a right but much more a social welfare measure directed towards the most needy or 'at risk'.[13] The lack of child care institutions means that mothers are expected to look after their children whether they have paid work or not, and consequently in Britain married women with small children have the lowest activity rates of all European countries.[14] It is ironic that at a time when the family is in greatest need of money, women have to give up their paid work. This has had serious effects on the economic well-being of families with small children and on single mothers, and, as a consquence, a large percentage of families with small children are living around or just above the official poverty line (Walker, Winyard and Pond, 1983).

## Women's dependency as workers, clients and consumers

The socio-economic changes in Britain during the last twenty years have been parallel to the developments in Denmark. There has been an expansion of women's involvement in paid work, which means that today the majority of women have become economically active, although many are in part-time jobs, and there has been a corresponding change in family form.

The rising proportion of single parents is another important characteristic of British society. In 1981, 11 per cent of all families with dependent children were one-parent families (i.e. approximately one in eight families), and eight out of nine lone parents were lone mothers. This development raises serious problems, because the social needs of these families cannot be met within the existing social security system, which makes lone mothers the exception to the 'typical' family form. As a result one-parent families have become grossly over-represented among the poor. It has been documented that half of all one-parent families have already become dependent for survival on some kind of state support, since, due to child care problems, they are generally unable to work full-time, and if they do work part-time, the wages will be deducted from the benefits received from the state.

The socio-economic and other changes in family form have made the contradictions in the social security system both more serious and more visible. Feminist analysis and reports from the Study Commission on the Family have shown that women have become involved in a sequence of caring responsibilities from children to parents and then spouses (Popay *et al.*, 1983; Rimmer, 1981; Rimmer and Popay, 1982). They conclude that given the changing socio-economic situation, it is not a realistic strategy to rely on women to take over more care work or to push more care work into the informal sector in the form of 'community care'. It will, on the contrary, become necessary for the state in the future to take over more responsibility from the families, organizing and funding care work.

In Britain, feminist scholars have been very critical of the welfare state, which has been characterized predominantly as an instrument for reproducing the unequal sexual division of work in society. They have documented that British social policies rest on consistent, though often hidden, assumptions about the division of unpaid labour in the home, and on assumptions about the different relation that men and women have to the labour market. These conceptions about the role of the family and women in society have become an important part of both legislation and administrative rules. In this way the dominant political forces have created an institutional structure, that have helped to maintain and reproduce the sexual division of labour and male domination. The conclusion is clearly that the state has not been neutral to women, but has favoured certain 'male' values over other 'female' values, and the interests of men rather than the interests of women. There is, however, no agreement about why the state has supported and protected the patriarchal family. Has the state served the interests of capital or the interests of patriarchy, or both? What has been the role of the Labour Movement? Why did the Labour Party hold on to the notion of the family-wage in spite of changing socio-economic conditions?

## The welfare state as a new form of patriarchal power?

There has been disagreement among feminist scholars about women's relation to the welfare state and about the nature of the state. The theoretical question about the nature of the state has often been reduced by feminists to a discussion about whether the state is capitalist or patriarchal or both. Feminists like Mary

McIntosh and Elizabeth Wilson have argued that the state is predominantly capitalist, because patriarchy in its old form, as family patriarchy, has been abolished, although there is still an oppression of women in the family, e.g., by the family-wage system. Other feminists like Zillah Eisenstein have argued that there has been a change in patriarchy from a family to a social patriarchy, in which the state plays an important role in reproducing patriarchal power. I have argued that the changes in male domination with the advance of the modern welfare state can be interpreted as a shift in the focus of oppression from the private to the public sphere. This still leaves open important questions about the nature of the modern welfare state and women's relation to the state. While I agree with Eisenstein about the changing character of women's oppression in the modern state, I find that she puts too much emphasis on the oppressive patriarchal character of the state. Her analysis is too much coloured by the liberal Anglo-Saxon state. The Danish (and Scandinavian) welfare state project is in important ways different from both the American and the British welfare states and these differences have been important for women.

Another important question has been whether the expansion of the welfare state has been primarily an expression of patriarchal interests dominating the decision-making process, or whether public policies have rather been the passive response to more general socio-economic changes, such as the growing demand in the economy for married women's labour power and the parallel decline of the one-earner family. The comparison between Denmark and other welfare states like Britain makes it clear that there is no simple economic determination at play. On the one hand, the socio-economic forces have in all welfare states resulted in an integration of married women into the labour market and a parallel decline of the one-earner family as the dominant family form. On the other hand, there has been ample room for different political forces to act as mediators between the socio-economic forces and the social needs and interests of different social groups. The argument that politics does make a difference does not necessarily mean that state policies have been primarily concerned to ensure male dominance. On the contrary, it makes it necessary to examine concrete policies in order to understand the political and social forces at play. State policies can finally be an expression of what has been called separate state interests, e.g., in economic growth, in securing an international position or in internal stability.[15]

In Denmark there has been a political consensus about the formulation of a welfare state project which included 'socializing reproduction' by building a network of social institutions which in the 1960s and 1970s has made care work part of social citizenship. There has no doubt been a mix of objectives behind these social policies. One objective has been to help the family as a social unit to survive under changing socio-economic conditions, another has been to help satisfy industry's growing need for a larger labour force, and a third objective has been to achieve a greater equality between families with and without children. In Britain there was, on the other hand, a political consensus between the Labour Party and the Conservative Party about a very different social policy with the purpose of preserving the one-earner family with a breadwinner and a dependent wife. In neither case have state policies been neutral towards women. In Denmark the state has, for a number of reasons, used its policies to help facilitate the integration of women in the public sphere via the expansion of a network of social services. In Britain, however, the state has failed to create such a network. Instead it has used its social policies to support the home-making role of women, and in this way the state in Britain became a major obstacle to the integration of women in the public sphere. In Britain legislation has been explicitly and openly discriminatory towards women, whereas in Denmark public policies have apparently been gender neutral. In neither case have the contradictions in women's situation between their dual roles as workers and mothers been abolished.

The development of the Danish welfare state has had very contradictory effects on women's social and economic position. On the one hand state support for a social service economy built on institutions for social care of children, the sick and the old has been very favourable for women. It has helped women to become part of the permanent work-force and has made it possible for them to support themselves through wage-work. In this sense it can be argued that a private patriarchal order has been partly replaced by a public order, which is formally 'gender-neutral', and that women have obtained more influence in the male-dominated sphere. In this sense it can be argued that the state has empowered women by providing a certain autonomy and freedom from male domination in the private sphere and a certain protection of the female values of care through the socialization of care work.[16] On the other hand this apparent gender neutrality in the public sphere has also become part of a new form of male domination, and women have been subsumed under a public power hierarchy. Male domination has clearly changed: it is important that sex *per se* is no longer regarded as a legitimate source of power, although there is still a strong male domination in the central spheres of economic and political life. This new form of male domination is radically different from the old form and has given women a better platform from which to attack male domination in both the public and the private sphere. One important question remains: how have these changes in male power influenced women's activities as citizens?

## Feminist strategies towards the welfare state in Denmark

It can be argued that the welfare state project has mobilized women politically and that women are becoming increasingly active as citizens in order to fight in different ways for their own interests. Today, when the welfare state has come under attack from different political quarters, gender has become a political issue because women's votes can make a difference and women's activities can influence the future development of the welfare state. In Denmark, women have in the past been objects of the political process and have not had control over power positions. This does not mean, however, that women have been unable to *influence* political issues through their political activities and through participation in informal organizations, like charity, religious organizations and in the Old Feminist movement.

In Denmark the Old Feminist Organization (Dansk Kvindesamfund + DK: The Danish Women's Society), formed in 1871, was a strong advocate of equal rights and equal opportunities for men and women and a supporter of the integration of women into the public sphere. The organization quite naturally became one of the strong supporters of the new formal equality policies of the 1960s and 1970s. DK was represented in the Government Commission which was set up in 1965 to investigate women's position in society. The reports from the Commission indicated a general consensus about the need for state support to increase married women's integration into the formal labour market through an expansion of part-time work, and an increase in public child care facilities. Although the organization in principle emphasized women's free choice between the home and the labour market, it nonetheless actively supported the new partnership between the state and the family, and the subsequent institutionalization of women's double role through the expansion of state responsibilities for care work. The organization wanted men to take a more active part in domestic work, but it never seriously challenged the sexual division of work in the family or in society. One of the main results of the Commission's work was the institutionalization of a public equality policy through the establishment of an Equality Council in 1975 with representatives from both economic interest organizations and women's organizations. The old feminists from different political parties shared the general belief that the struggle for greater equality between men and women would be achieved step by step through parliamentary reform. This consensus was not seriously challenged until the rise of the New Feminist Movement in 1970.

The New Feminist Movement (the Redstockings) challenged the old feminists on all crucial issues. The New Movement (NFM) was an anti-capitalist movement, seeing women's struggle as part of the struggle of the working-class for socialism. The objective of the struggle was not greater equality between men and women, but emancipation and the abolition of the sexual division of labour and male dominance both in the family and in society. The New Feminist Movement was, in contrast to the old feminist organization, a non-hierarchical collectively organized movement engaged primarily in extra-parliamentary activities. The goal was no longer to obtain power in the male-dominated institutions, but rather to increase women's collective consciousness and to change people's minds, as a precondition for changing social institutions.

In Denmark the New Feminist Movement has from the start been ambivalent about the modern welfare state. On the one hand, the NFM was the first to break the consensus and criticize the welfare state for its oppression of women in the family and in society. At a theoretical level, the NFM opposed the state as a patriarchal and hierarchical institution. However, in practice the feminist movement has been a passive and rather uncritical supporter of the actual expansion of the institutions of social services and the socialization of care work, concentrating on quantitative demands for more social services free of charge and to a lesser extent on qualitative demands. At the beginning of the 1970s the differences between the old and the new women's movements were profound, but with the economic crisis, growing unemployment and cuts in the social services and benefits, women from the different organizations have gradually become united around demands to maintain and improve the level of existing social services and welfare benefits, and demands to improve women's situation in the labour market and create greater equal opportunities for women in the public sphere of work and politics. Today one of the most important demands for all feminists has become the demand for a shorter working day and the abolition of the sexual division of labour in the labour market and in the family.

The New Feminist Movement has not controlled power positions, but it has to some extent been able to influence the political issues. There is a general agreement that the ideological influence of the NFM has been especially strong in Denmark.[17] The ideas from the New Feminist Movement about the abolition of the sexual division of labour in the family and society have spread far beyond the original organization. Today only a small number of women are still actively engaged in the New Feminist Movement, but feminists from the NFM have instead become actively engaged in changing existing institutions through all kinds of political activity in trade unions, the social movements and in the political parties of the Left (Dahlerup, 1984). It is apparently a paradox that the institutionalization of equality policies has taken place parallel to the growth of the ideological influence of the NFM which had quite different goals. It has been argued that there has been an indirect connection between these apparently contradictory factors, in the sense that the ideas of the NFM have helped to strengthen the women (and men) working for an official equality policy even though the new feminists did not at the time actively support these policies themselves (Dahlerup and Guli, 1985, pp. 8–58).

## Women's political mobilization as citizens

During the last twenty years the Danish welfare state has witnessed a growing political mobilization and radicalization of women in all spheres of life. For the first time in history women have become as politically active as men, and today women actually vote in the same numbers as men. Research from Denmark indicates that there is no longer any difference between the extent of political activity of young men and women, but there is still a significant difference in their political profile, i.e., in the type of activity that they are engaged in. Young women are more active than men in the new social movements and in the trade unions (though not at the top level), while young men are more active than women in political parties and at public meetings (Togeby, 1984).

There are still significant differences between the participation of women and men in the three different political arenas of the electoral bodies, the corporate bodies and the political movements. There has, however, been a rapid increase in female representation in the legislative bodies during the 1960s and 1970s, and today in the Scandinavian countries women's representation in the parliamentary bodies is the highest in the world. In Denmark the percentage of women in Parliament has risen from 10 per cent in 1960 to 26 per cent in 1985. While the increase in female representation is important and has certainly given women more influence in Parliament, it does not necessarily follow that women have obtained more real power over political decision-making and the actual administration of the welfare state. This is because during the same period, the relative power of Parliament has declined as a result of growing corporatism; this corporatism has changed the institutional structure of the state and has increased the power both of economic organisations and administrators *vis-à-vis* Parliament. There is no doubt that this has made it more difficult for women to wield power over important political decisions (Hernes and Hanninen-Salmelin, 1985, pp. 155–92; Hernes, 1987, Chapter 4). Thus the ideas of the old and new women's movements have spread well beyond those movements, while, at the same time, the power position of women over the general domain of politics has remained relatively static, or even declined.

## Britain: the New Right, women and the family

In Britain there was during the 1940s and 1950s a political consensus about support for the family and traditional family values. Women of different classes supported the idea of women's home-making role, and there was a strong sense of domesticity among both men and women in the working-class (Campbell, 1984).[18] The Women's Liberation Movement (WLM), like the NFM in Denmark, developed in the late 1960s and the early 1970s in a welfare state governed at the time by a Labour Party. The WLM was influenced by the Labour movement and it has been argued that the strong familist and paternalist ideology and practice in the Labour movement made the WLM strongly suspicious of a centralized leadership and organization and also critical towards both the Labour Party and the centralized Trades Union Congress (TUC). The WLM in contrast to the Danish movement focused on the oppressive role of the family, and the family wage, and campaigned for more resources to women in the family as carers. More specifically, feminists in Britain have voiced a strong criticism of the economism of the Labour Movement, which they claim to be connected with men's belief in their role as breadwinners and an expression of their self-interest as breadwinners.[19]

During the 1980s new policies of privatization, domestification and the revival of the private sector have been advocated as part of the general strategy to restructure the welfare state under the Conservative administration led by Margaret Thatcher. These policies all attempt to shift some state responsibilities from the public sector to the market sphere, or to the family and the community. They can be interpreted as a new form of familism, where one of the goals has clearly been to allow the family and the community to play a larger role in the organization of care work, and there has been an appeal to women as mothers to take over more responsibility for care work and support the ideas about community care. The new Conservative policies hit women hard both as public service workers, as mothers and consumers of social services and as clients in the social system. It has, however, been argued that Thatcherism as an ideology is rather ambivalent towards women. On the one hand, there has been a recognition of women's care work as part of the third domestic welfare system located in the family and the community. On the other hand, the social and economic policies of the Thatcher administration have made it more difficult for most women to carry out their jobs as mothers in their daily lives, because of growing unemployment among their husbands and growing poverty among families with small children.[20]

How have women responded to this new familism? Although Thatcherism has supported traditional family values and has appealed to women as mothers, there is no clear evidence that there has been a greater swing of women than men to the Conservative Party. Many women have supported welfare benefits and services, and women organized in the Trade Union Movement have actually been among the most active and outspoken critics against the political programme of the New Right. Other women have organized as carers and fought for more resources for informal carers at home. Women organized as service workers in the National Union of Public Employees (NUPE) and the National Association of Local Government Officers (NALGO) have been trying to develop new strategies towards the struggle against privatization and domestification based on consumer needs and on an alliance between producers of social services and consumers and clients. These new strategies have today become a challenge to both the TUC and the Labour Party.[21]

## Challenges from a feminist perspective

In this article I have argued that politics do make a difference, and that differences in the political cultures and institutional structures in Denmark and Britain have influenced women's different roles as workers, mothers and citizens. The historical differences in both the values and policies of the Danish and the British Labour Movement have gradually become part of the institutional structure and political culture of the modern welfare state. The socio-economic changes during the last twenty years have in both countries changed the role of the family and the role of women in society, but the dominant political forces have reacted differently towards this new situation. In Denmark there has been a broad political consensus about a new organization of care work and a new understanding of women as 'working mothers', and this has helped to accelerate the integration of women into the public sphere of work and to hasten the changes in family forms. In contrast the social and family policies in Britain have delayed the integration of women into the work-force and have supported the unequal division of work in the family.

In Denmark the Social Democratic welfare project has in

important ways improved women's economic and social situation both as mothers and workers. The state has facilitated women's integration in the public sphere and has to a large extent helped women to become economically self-sufficient through the expansion of the public service sector. On the other hand, the Social Democratic form of welfare has also been paternalistic towards women, in the sense that women have not been able to determine their own interests but have predominantly been objects in the political process. This is the basis for the argument that the welfare state project has not abolished male dominance but has rather helped to strengthen male domination in the public sphere of work and politics. One of the unintended effects of the strong growth of the public sector has actually been to exacerbate the sexual division of labour in society.

Women's dependency on the state is not in itself a problem. In contemporary capitalism there is no alternative to women's dependency on the state. Historically the alternative was the economic dependency of the wife on her husband. The socio-economic changes during the last twenty years have in all welfare states made women dependent on different sources of income. Moreover, it is wrong *per se* to associate a strong welfare sector, like the Danish, with strong dependency on the state. For women it is actually the other way around: a strong public service sector seems to be a precondition for entry into the labour market, and thus avoiding becoming solely dependent on the state as clients. In Denmark, and Sweden, women have come to rely on the state primarily as workers and consumers of public services, and only to a small degree as clients. The opposite is true in Britain and in the United States where women to a greater extent have come to support themselves and their children by relying solely on family relationships or on the labour market.

While I have argued that the Danish welfare project has improved women's lives as workers, mothers and citizens, this does not mean that the Scandinavian countries can be used, as in many comparative studies, as an ideal model to secure women's equality, using either the strong position of Labour ideas in society and the subsequent strong integration of women as workers, or on the basis of the strong 'social state'. In contrast I have found that women's position cannot be measured solely by their relative position in the labour market, nor by the explicit policies of the state. A feminist analysis of the welfare state must study the interrelation of the different systems of welfare provided by state institutions, the labour market, and the family, because each represents different ways of organizing and satisfying human needs.

During the 1970s the contradictions in the situation of women in modern welfare states have been sharpened. During the economic crisis and mass unemployment there has been a growing marginalization of especially old and young unskilled women in the labour market and an exacerbation of the sexual division of labour. On the other hand, there has been an unprecedented mobilization of women as political actors fighting for their own interests. Women's growing political activities as citizens have in some cases made women the strongest defenders of the welfare state. In spite of the important divisions among women, all women have increasingly come to rely directly or indirectly on the state for support as workers employed in the public sector, as consumers dependent on social services or as clients dependent on welfare benefits. This is the material basis for the growing political solidarity among different groups of women in Scandinavia, and the background to the attempts to form alliances between women as producers of public services and as consumers and clients. The changes in the form of male power have today made it more important than ever that women strive to be present within the public institutions and to develop strategies towards the welfare state and towards the organization of care work. There seems to be a growing awareness among feminists that women's integration into public institutions has today become one precondition for influencing the values, political priorities and the actual policies of public institutions.

## Notes

1. See for example Zillah Eisenstein (1981), Lydia Sargent (1981) and Michelle Barrett (1980).
2. See Mary Ruggie (1984) and Carolyn Teich Adams and Katryn Teich Winston (1980). The two books are examples of comparative studies that both, in different ways, touch upon women's relation to the state.
3. This paper is built both on a study on women's integration in the Danish welfare state with Anette Borchorst (see Anette Borchorst and Birte Siim (1987)) and on my own comparative work on women and the

welfare state in Denmark, Britain and the United States. See Birte Siim (1985 and 1988).

4. I have in my work been inspired by Helga Hernes' studies of women's dependence on the state as employees, clients and citizens. In my own studies I have a somewhat different approach that emphasizes the relationship between women's different roles as mothers, workers and citizens. (See Helga Hernes, 1984.)

5. The term familism has been defined by Michelle Barrett and Mary McIntosh (1982) as 'the propagation of politically pro-family ideas and the strengthening of families themselves' as distinct from familization, 'ideologies modelled on what are thought to be family values and the rendering of other social phenomena like families'. I use familism in a more specific way to designate ideas and policies that strengthen a specific family form with a breadwinner and a homemaker. This makes my definition of the term different from the notion of family policy (see note 12).

6. For the analysis of the Scandinavian welfare states I build especially on the works of the Swedish sociologist Gøran Therborn and of Gøsta Esping-Andersen. See for example Gøran Therborn (1986 and 1987) and Gøsta Esping-Andersen (1980, 1981, 1983, 1984 and 1985). My approach is, however, somewhat different from theirs for reasons that I develop in the following.

7. Helga Maria Hernes has taken up this question in her latest book (1987, p. 11). She argues that the Scandinavian welfare states have empowered women more than other political systems. We need, however, to define more precisely what we mean by empowering.

8. See especially Therborn (1986). In a later article Therborn stresses the need for more qualitative and comparative welfare state studies (1987).

9. In Denmark the Liberals and the Right in contrast to Sweden and Norway actually prohibited the passing of old age pensions (ATP) dependent on previous incomes and financed partly by the employers organizations that the Social Democratic Party wanted. See Gøsta Esping-Andersen (1980).

10. For a more detailed analysis of the day care policies in Denmark see Anette Borchorst, this volume.

11. For a more detailed account of the changes in women's position as workers, consumers and clients during the last twenty years, see Anette Borchorst and Birte Siim (1987).

12. The study of the role of the family in the organization of social reproduction in Britain relies to a large extent on the works of and personal contacts with a number of feminist researchers, among others Elizabeth Wilson, Hilary Land and Hilary Rose, Miriam David, Clare Ungerson and Mary McIntosh, and on the different reports from the Study Commission on the family.

13. Hilary Land (1980). See also Mary Ruggie (1981).
14. Activity rates are defined as the number of economically active persons per 100 persons in relation to all persons in different groups.
15. For a discussion of these separate state interests see also Vicki Randall (1982, pp. 129–30).
16. Helga Maria Hernes (1987, p. 31) has argued that there is an important difference between being powerless and having little power.
17. In Drude Dahlerup and Britta Guli's article *The Impact of Women's Liberation Movement on Public Policy in Denmark and Norway* (1983), they study the influence of the Women's Liberation Movement (WLM) on the two issues of free abortion and the Equal Treatment Act.
18. For the differences between the NFM in Britain and other countries see Jane Jensen (1983, pp. 341–75).
19. Elizabeth Wilson analyses in her book (1982) the post-war changes in the ideals for housewives and shows that there was a conscious attempt by the Labour Party to give women's homemaking role a new status.
20. The relationship between Thatcherism and women is discussed by Jean Gardiner (1983), Lynne Segal (1983), Hilary and Steven Rose (1982), and by Miriam David (1983, pp. 31–45).
21. Material from NUPE and personal talks with Sue Slipman, former organizer and administrator in NUPE during the spring of 1984.

# References

Adams, C. T. and Winston, K. T. (1980), *Mothers at Work: Public policies in the US, Sweden and Britain* (New Jersey: Princeton University Press)
Andersen, B. R. (1983a), *Two Essays on the Nordic Welfare States* (Copenhagen: Amtskommunerne og Kommunernes forskningsinstitution)
Andersen, B. R. (1983b), 'Den danske velfærdsstat-vækst og krise' ('The Danish welfare state – growth and crisis'), in *Økonomi og politik* ('Economics and Politics') no. 1
Andersen, B. R. (1984), *Kan vi bevare Vefærdsstaten* ('Can we preserve the welfare state?') (Copenhagen: Amtskummunernes Forskningsinstitut)
Barrett, M. (1980), *Women's Oppression Today* (London: New Left Books)
Barrett, M. and McIntosh, M. (1980), 'The family wage: some problems for socialists and feminists', *Capital and Class* 11, Summer
Barrett, M. and McIntosh, M. (1982), *The Anti-Social Family* (London: Verso)
Borchorst, A. and Siim, B. (1984), *Kvinder og velfærdsstaten- mellem*

*moderskab og lønarbejde i 100 år* ('Women and the welfare state – between motherhood and wagework in 100 years') (Aalborg: Aalborg University Press)

Borchorst, A. and Siim, B. (1987), 'Women and the advanced welfare state: towards a new kind of patriarchal power?', in A. Showstack Sassoon (ed.), *Women and the State: The shifting boundaries between public and private* (London: Hutchinson)

Dale, J. and Foster, P. (1986), *Feminists and State Welfare* (London: Routledge and Kegan Paul)

Campbell, B. (1984), *Wigan Pier Revisited* (London: Virago)

Campbell, B. and Coote, A. (1982), *Sweet Freedom: The struggle for women's liberation* (London: Pan)

David, M. (1983), 'Sexual morality and the New Right', *Critical Social Policy* vol. 2, no. 3

Dahlerup, D. (1984), *Is the New Women's Liberation Movement Dead?* (Aarhus, Denmark: Institute of Political Science, University of Aarhus)

Dahlerup, Drude and Guli, Britta (1983), *The Impact of Women's Liberation Movement on Public Policy in Denmark and Norway* (Aarhus, Denmark: University of Aarhus, Institute of Political Science)

Dahlerup, D. and Guli, B. (1985), 'Kvindeorganisationer i Norden: Afmagt eller modmagt? ('Feminist Organizations in the Nordic Countries'), in E. Haavio-Manila (ed.), *Unfinished Democracy: Women in Nordic Politics* (Oxford: Pergamon Press)

Eisenstein, Zillah (1981), *The Radical Future of Liberal Feminism* (New York: Longman)

Eisenstein, Zillah (1983), 'The state, the patriarchal family and working mothers', in I. Diamond (ed.), *Families, Politics and Public Policy: A feminist dialogue on women and the state* (New York: Longman)

Eisenstein, Zillah (1984), *Feminism and Sexual Equality: Crisis in liberal feminism* (New York: Monthly Review Press)

Esping-Andersen, G. (1980), *Social class, Social Democracy and State Policy* (Copenhagen: New Social Science Monograph)

Esping-Andersen, G. (1981), *Politics Against Markets: Decommodification in Social Policy*, paper presented at the Arne Ryde Symposium on the Economics of Social Security, Lund

Esping-Andersen, G. (1983), 'After the welfare state', *Public Welfare*, Winter

Esping-Andersen, G. (1984), *The State as a System of Stratification: Capitalism, liberalism, and socialism in the organization of social welfare programs* (First draft of a working paper, Harvard)

Esping-Andersen, G. (1985), *Politics Against Markets* (New Jersey: Princeton University Press)

Gardiner, J. (1983), 'Women, recession and the Tories', in S. Hall,

M. Jacques (eds.), *The Politics of Thatcherism* (London: Lawrence and Wishart)

Geckler, S. (1982) *Notat om enlige mødres arbejds- og leveforhold* ('Paper on single mothers' working and living conditions') (The Danish National Institute of Social Research, March)

Gough, I. (1977), *The Political Economy of the Welfare State* (London: Macmillan)

Hartman, H. (1979), 'Capitalism, patriarchy and job segregation by sex', in Z. Eisenstein (ed.), *The Capitalist Patriarchy and the Case for Socialist Feminism* (New York: Monthly Review Press)

Hernes, H. (1984), 'Women and the welfare state: the transition from private to public dependence', in H. Holler (ed.), *Patriarchy in a Welfare Society* (Oslo: Universitetsforlaget)

Hernes, H. (1987), *Welfare State and Women Power: Essays in state feminism* (Norway: Norwegian University Press)

Hernes, H. and Hanninen-Salmelin, E. (1985), 'Kvinders repræsentation i det korporative system' ('Women's representation in the corporate system'), in E. Haavio-Manila (ed.), *Unfinished Democracy: Women in Nordic politics* (Oxford: Pergamon Press)

Jensen, J. (1983), 'The modern women's movement in Italy, France, and Great Britain: Differences in life cycles', *Comparative Social Research*, vol. 5

Jonasdottir, A. (1985), 'Kvinnors interessen och andra værden' ('Women's interests and other values'), *Kvinnovetenskaplig Tidsskrift*, no. 2

Jørgensen, W. (1985), *Enlige forsørgere i bistandssystemet* ('Single supporters in the system of social welfare') (The Danish National Institute of Social Research, July)

Kamerman, S. and A. Kahn (eds.) (1978), *Family Policy, Government and Families in Fourteen Countries* (New York: Columbia University Press)

Land, H. (1978), 'Who cares for the family?', *Journal of Social Policy*, vol. 7, part 3

Land, H. (1980), 'The family wage', *Feminist Review*, no. 6

Logue, J. (1968), 'Social welfare, equality and the Labour Movement in Denmark, and Sweden', *Comparative Social Research*, vol. 6

Marcussen, R. (1980), 'Socialdemokratiet, velfærdsstaten og kvinderne' ('Social Democratic Party, the welfare state and women'), *Den jyske Historiker*, no. 18

Marshall, T. H. (1983), 'Citizenship and social class', in D. Held (ed.), *States and Societies* (Oxford: Martin Robertson, in association with Open University Press)

McIntosh, M. (1979), 'The state and the oppression of women', in A. Kuhn and A. Wolpe (eds.), *Feminism and Materialism* (London: Routledge)

Olesen, H. (1973), *Ældre på pleje- og alderdomshjem* ('Old people living in

Nursing and Old age homes, with an English summary') The Danish National Institute of Social Research, no. 57 (Copenhagen)

Olesen, Henning (1981), *De Ældres Vilkår* ('The Conditions of the Elderly'), Aeldrekommissions 2, delrappart, April

Olesen, H., Trampe, J. P. and Hansen, G. (1976), *Familiekontakter i den tidlige alderdom* ('Family contacts in the early stages of old age, with an English summary'), The Danish National Institute of Social Research, no. 74 (Copenhagen)

Popay, J., Rimmer, L. and Rossiter, C. (1983), *One-Parent Families, Children and Public Policy*, The Study Commission on the Family, Occasional Paper, no. 12

Randall, V. (1982), *Women and Politics* (London: Macmillan)

Rimmer, L. (1981), *Families in Focus: marriage, divorce and family patterns*, The Study Commission on the Family, Occasional Paper, no. 6

Rimmer, L. and Popay, J. (1982), *Employment Trends and the Family*, The Study Commission on the Family, Occasional Paper, no. 10

Rose, H. and Rose, S. (1982), 'Moving right out of welfare – and the way back', *Critical Social Policy*, vol. 2, no. 1

Ruggie, M. (1981), 'Public day care in Britain and Sweden', in N. Black and A. B. Cattrell (eds.), *Women and World Change: Equity issues in development* (London: Sage Publications)

Ruggie, M. (1984), *The State and Working Women: A comparative study of Britain and Sweden* (New Jersey: Princeton University Press)

Sargent, Lydia (ed.) (1981), *Women and Revolution* (Boston: South End Press)

Segal, L. (1983), 'The heat in the kitchen', in S. Hall and M. Jacques (eds.), *Politics of Thatcherism* (London: Lawrence and Wishart)

Siim, B. (1985), *Women and the Welfare State: Between Private and Public Dependence*, Working paper (The Centre for Research on Women, Stanford University)

Siim, B. (1987), 'The Scandinavian welfare states: Towards sexual equality or a new kind of male domination?' *Acta Sociologica*, vol. 30, nos. 3–4

Siim, B. (1988), 'Towards a feminist rethinking of the Welfare State', in A. Jonasdottir and K. Jones (eds.), *The Political Interest of Gender: Developing theory and research with a feminist face* (London: Sage)

Therborn, G. (1986), 'Classes and states: Welfare states developments 1881–1981', in P. Kettunen (ed.), Papers on Labour History, *Det nordiske i den nordiske arbetaroralsen* ('The Nordic in the Nordic Labour Movement') (Helsinki: The Finnish Society for Labour History and Cultural Traditions)

Therborn, G. (1987), 'Welfare states and capitalist markets' in *Acta Sociologica*, vol. 30, nos. 3–4

Togeby, L. (1984), *Politik er også en kvindesag* ('Politics is also a female concern') (Aarhus Universitet: Politica)

Ungerson, C. (ed.) (1985), *Women and Social Policy: A reader* (London: Macmillan)

Vedel-Petersen, J. (1978), 'Denmark', in S. Kamerman and A. Kahn (eds.), *Family Policy: Government and families in fourteen countries* (New York: Columbia University Press)

Walker, A., Winyard, S. and Pond, C. (1983), 'Conservative economic policy: The social consequences' in D. Bull and P. Wilding (eds.), *Thatcherism and the Poor*, The Child Poverty Action Group, Poverty Pamphlet, no. 59

Wilson, E. (1977), *Women and the Welfare State* (London: Tavistock)

Wilson, E. (1982), *Only Half-Way to Paradise: Women in post-war Britain, 1945–68* (London: Tavistock)

# CHAPTER 6

# INFORMAL AND FORMAL CARE IN OLD AGE

## What is wrong with the new ideology in Scandinavia today?

KARI WÆRNESS

Marianne Weber said of her husband Max Weber that he 'was moved above all by the fact that on its earthly course an idea always and everywhere operates in opposition to its original meaning and thereby destroys itself' (Weber, 1975, p. 337). This statement can, in my opinion, epitomize the course taken by the concept 'community care' in the social policy of the Scandinavian welfare states today.

Concepts such as 'community care', 'self-care', 'integration' and 'normalization', which in an expansive phase of the welfare state could function as an ambitious ideology behind the development of new and better social services, can acquire quite another function against the background of an impending financial crisis in the public sector and of important changes in the needs of the dependants. The ideology of community care as both cheaper and morally preferable to institutional care, may, on the administrative and political level, function as a defence, or even as a positive evaluation of the difficulties of providing institutional care or other resource demanding social services to dependent people in greatest need of care. In such a way this ideology may result in the problems of the most helpless and disabled members of society becoming invisible in social planning and social policy.

The elderly are the largest group to which this ideology of community care is addressed. In spite of the fact that the waiting-lists for institutional care are steadily increasing, the attention both in research and governmental reports on the problems of old age care is, to an overwhelming degree, directed towards finding remedies to decrease the demand for institutional care.

The lack of knowledge about women both in welfare state policy and welfare state research is one reason behind the enthusiasm with which the idea of community care has been taken up in policy and research. The fact that women's studies during recent years have uncovered parts of the 'invisible world' of women in a way that is about to change our perceptions and theories about the welfare state, has hitherto had very little influence on social planning and policy in the field of care for the elderly. Government authorities have during the last decade insisted that greater equality between the sexes is an important political goal. The same holds for the aim of strengthening informal caring networks. The problem of how to find political measures which do not make these aims contradictory has still not been seriously discussed. Elucidations of the conditions and consequences of the policy of community care are therefore important both for social policy and as a feminist question.

In the following paper I will use some recent empirical data to argue that this new policy of 'community care' is based on myths rather than realities concerning the situation and preferences of elderly people and on an outdated understanding of women's roles in family and society. Abandoning the myths and using a more realistic comprehension of women's situation is a necessary, if not a sufficient, condition for a future-oriented social policy better fitted to make the above-mentioned political aims more consistent. In many ways it may seem Utopian to envisage a future in which the care of the elderly and handicapped is no longer dependent on women's subordinate position in society, but it seems that there is still some possibility for reform within the context of the Scandinavian welfare states.

## Four myths about 'community care' for the elderly

As a number of studies in recent years have suggested, 'caring' is a concept which needs to be analysed and defined more precisely in order to elucidate some of the crucial issues for social policy in the welfare state today. (See for instance Graham, 1983; Ungerson,

1983; Wærness, 1984a and 1984b.)[1] In this paper I will primarily relate the discussion to problems connected with the caring of the frail elderly (i.e., to the elderly who cannot manage on their own in everyday life) and the involvement of people who take on active caring on a consistent and reliable basis. This kind of caring is part of what I have defined as *care-giving work*, whether it is paid or not, no matter whether it takes place in the public or the private sphere (Wærness, 1984a). Care-giving work is a question of feelings, but even more it is a question of practical work carried out through looking after those who, temporarily or permanently, cannot manage on their own.

The first myth about the situation of the elderly today is that an increasing proportion is cared for in public institutions and that consequently there is scope for moving more responsibility from the public to the private sector. Table 6.1 shows that the institutionalization rates in both Sweden and Norway have been nearly constant or have slightly decreased in the last decade. As for the number of disabled elderly living outside institutions compared to the number living in institutions, we do not have studies or statistics which we can use as the basis to make strict comparisons. However, from what evidence we do have, it seems reasonable to conclude that the majority of the frail elderly live outside institutions. For

**Table 6.1** Percentage of the young-old (65–79 years) and the old-old (80 years and over) living in institutions in Norway and Sweden in the period 1970–82 (estimated numbers[1]).

|  | Young-old (65–79 years) | | Old-old (80 years and over) | |
|---|---|---|---|---|
|  | Norway | Sweden | Norway | Sweden |
| 1970 | 2.9 | 3.7 | 20.1 | 27.4 |
| 1975 | 2.7 | 3.2 | 20.9 | 26.8 |
| 1980 | 2.5 | 2.7 | 21.8 | 25.0 |
| 1982 | 2.5 | 2.4 | 21.8 | 24.6 |

*Note*: [1]The numbers are based partly on statistics for the whole population of pensioners and patients, and partly on surveys. It has been necessary to adjust the numbers. The numbers shown here are therefore not exact, but approximately correct, and the trend should be correct.
*Source*: Daatland and Sundstrøm, 1985.

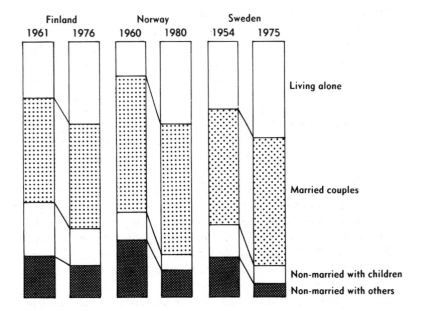

**Figure 6.1** The household structure of the non-institutionalized elderly population (65 and over) in Scandinavia, 1954–80 (percentages). Note that some of the married couples' households also consist of children. Most of these households consist of young-old people where children are relatively young and still have not moved out of their parents' households. The non-married living with children are older, and in these households the child often will be the 'main person' in the household. (*Source*: Daatland and Sundstrøm, 1985)

example, in the Norwegian Survey of Housing Conditions, 12 per cent of the elderly (aged 65 and over) reported that they were in need of nursing, and in addition 14 per cent reported that they were disabled (Ås, 1984). As we know from a number of studies, the likelihood of being institutionalized in old age depends on the individual's household situation, civil status and whether or not he or she has children. Figure 6.1 shows how the household structure of the non-institutionalized elderly population in Scandinavia has changed in the period 1954–80. The number of people living alone has increased considerably, the proportion of households with

**Table 6.2**  The household structure of the non-institutionalized elderly population (65 and over) in Norway, 1981, percentages according to sex and age.

| | Living alone | Living with spouse | Living with spouse and children | Living with children | Living with siblings | Other kind of household | Total |
|---|---|---|---|---|---|---|---|
| Men | 20 | 56 | 11 | 5 | 5 | 4 | 100 |
| Women | 45 | 29 | 4 | 11 | 7 | 3 | 100 |
| Age groups | | | | | | | |
| 65–9 years | 24 | 55 | 7 | 7 | 5 | 3 | 100 |
| 70–4 years | 32 | 44 | 7 | 6 | 7 | 4 | 100 |
| 75–9 years | 50 | 25 | 8 | 8 | 8 | 1 | 100 |
| 80+ years | 44 | 21 | 5 | 15 | 6 | 9 | 100 |
| All | 35 | 40 | 7 | 8 | 6 | 4 | 100 |

*Source*: Norwegian Survey of Housing Conditions 1981, reported in Ås, 1984.

elderly spouses also shows some increase, while it has become less common to live in households with children.

As shown in Table 6.2, the household structure of elderly men and women is considerably different. This difference is part of the explanation of the fact that the institutionalization rate for elderly women is so much higher than for men. The spouse is the most important care-giver for frail elderly men. Table 6.3 gives some impression of the differences between the sexes in this respect. In addition to far more women having to care for disabled and ill husbands, disabled husbands need more care than disabled wives, and care-giving wives far less frequently receive any help from people or organizations than do care-giving husbands.

Different studies of inter-generational care in the family show that it is first and foremost daughters who do the care-giving work, especially the particularly demanding tasks, including intimate physical care (Daatland, 1983; Nygård, 1982; Rø *et al.*, 1983). Even if some sons also take responsibility for frail elderly parents (very often with a great deal of help from their wives), it still seems to be true that the probability of being institutionalized in old age is dependent on whether or not you have a daughter (Nygård, 1982).

**Table 6.3a** Percentage of the age group 65–74 years who had or had had a spouse who needed extra nursing, supervision or help because of chronic illness, disabilities or old age.

|  | Men | Women |
|---|---|---|
| Having a dependent spouse for the time being | 7 | 15 |
| Had a dependent spouse earlier, but no longer | 8 | 8 |
| Percentage of the care-giving spouses having any help from others | 43 | 10 |

*Source*: Norwegian Time Budget Survey 1980–1, reported in Longsom, 1984.

**Table 6.3b** Percentage of the dependent spouses who needed different kinds of helping activities.

|  | Wife dependent | Husband dependent |
|---|---|---|
| Needed help in connection with: |  |  |
| meals | 22 | 32 |
| dressing and undressing | 17 | 62 |
| personal hygiene | 30 | 74 |
| supervision the whole day | 9 | 26 |
| supervision part of the day | 44 | 47 |
| moving indoors | 22 | 35 |
| moving outdoors | 61 | 47 |
| | $N = (23)$ | (34) |

From Figure 6.2 we can conclude that the importance of the public home-help services in realizing the goal of community care for the elderly has increased in all Scandinavian countries since the mid-1960s. Both from survey data and from different qualitative studies we know that a very high proportion of the clients receiving home-help services are in addition dependent on considerable informal care-giving work which is mainly done by daughters or

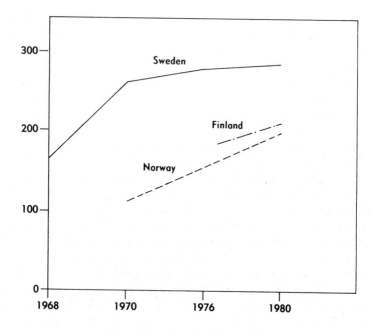

**Figure 6.2** Numbers per thousand households with at least one elderly person aged 65 and over (in Norway 67 years and over) who received public home help services in Scandinavia, 1965–82. (*Source*: Daatland and Sundstrøm, 1985)

other close female relatives (Wærness, 1982 and 1983; Sundstrøm, 1983; Nvgård, 1982; Rø *et al.*, 1983; Widding Isaksen, 1983).

It should be important for the people planning our social policy to realize the fact that community care is not a futuristic idea but that it is very much the reality of today's welfare state. On the basis of the Norwegian Time Budget Survey, Lingsom (1985) has calculated that all Norwegians in the age group 16–74 years give an amount of informal care to handicapped, ill and disabled people equivalent to 104,000 working-years in paid work (a working-year is defined as 1,900 hours). Compared to working-years spent on public home-care services, this informal effort is approximately eight times higher than the public effort.

The family is still the most important provider of care in old age, and the majority of the elderly who receive some form of public care live in the community and benefit from various combinations of public and private care. For many different reasons, some of which will be discussed later, it seems doubtful that there is much room for moving more responsibility to the family. On the contrary it seems more reasonable to expect a decrease in the family's capacity for care-giving work for the elderly.

A second myth is that, historically, the situation of the elderly has deteriorated. Social gerontology abounds with introductions concerning the declining situation of old people in modern society, 'displaced from the patriarchal eminence of the respectful village' (Stearns, 1977, p. 1). Recent historical studies show that this general image of pre-industrial Europe as a golden age for the elderly is a myth. (See for instance Mitterauer and Sieder, 1982; Stearns, 1977.) Sociologists have misunderstood the changes in family structure because of their pre-conceptions of the family in terms of kinship, reproduction, and biology, and because of their all too easy acceptance of the family as a final social unity, the building block of society (Laslett, 1982). Historical studies also make us aware that most social theories about the effects of modernization on the situation of the aged are not theories about the elderly *per se*, but mainly concern relatively well-off elderly men, who in former times mostly owned or controlled property on which younger people were dependent. Focusing on women and the lower classes, the transformation brought about by industrialization and urbanization of the problems of ageing becomes much more difficult to describe and to evaluate in terms of welfare.

From these new historical studies there emerges an image of very different family forms in pre-industrial societies. This means that the problems of ageing and how these have changed with the modernization of society cannot adequately be presented by simple comparisons of pre-industrial versus industrial conditions and mentalities. The myth of a golden past should be abandoned because it tends to imprison our own generation, preventing us from adapting caring institutions to our own contemporary purposes. From many studies of modern gerontology we also have to conclude that we should avoid far-reaching generalizations as to the problems of ageing in modern society. Education, socialization processes, socio-economic status, residential area, and income define different situations for men and women in varying family situations, which result in dissimilar behaviours and adjustments in old age.

In the current crisis of the modern welfare state, however, it seems important to emphasize that pension systems and social services have improved both the material and the social situation for most of the elderly. For one thing, the mass of the elderly have a much better private economy than that of former generations, and this of course is to a large extent a result of social security. But the importance of social security for the elderly is not only that it allows them a higher level of consumption, but also that it gives them a kind of independence they did not previously have. In modern society both the younger and the older generations seem to prefer to live in separate households, in what Rosenmayr and Køckeis (1965) have termed 'intimacy at a distance'. Little is known about preferences in earlier periods, but, in Scandinavia at least, separate households for the older and the younger generations in the family go a long way back. In the traditional peasant economy old people retired to a small house reserved for them in the neighbourhood of the farm, or to separate rooms in the house. Only on the poorest farms or when the old could not manage on their own, because of bad health or widowhood, did the generations live in the same household.

The improvement of pension systems during recent years has made it possible for a growing proportion of the elderly to manage on their own and not be completely dependent on close kin. The expansion of the public home-help services for the non-institutionalized elderly seems to have had the same effect (Sundstrøm, 1983; Daatland, 1983).

The decrease in co-residence rates between the generations (as shown in Figure 1) can be interpreted as an increasing possibility for the elderly to realize this preference for 'intimacy at a distance'. Since 1960 the Scandinavian countries have had a flat-rate non-contributory old-age pension which has risen faster than the incomes of the working population, and a growing proportion of the elderly (mostly men) have acquired the right to a supplementary earnings-related pension. Due to better pensions, better housing and the growth of public home-help services, the generations in the family have become less dependent on each other. Rather than evaluating this development as a kind of alienation of the elderly from their children, it should be seen as an improvement of the quality of the relationships between the generations (Shanas, 1979). Increased independence generally is taken to imply improved social status. It seems inconsistent that whilst we value economic independence with regard to the elderly, we seem too easily to be attracted to policies which imply dependency on private help and services.

A third myth dominating social gerontology is that the elderly are a homogeneous group and that their situation and problems are dominated by the fact (or shock) of retirement from working life. Shock or trauma may well be an appropriate description for a situation where income falls by a great deal. However, the perspective adopted is very often that it is the loss of work itself which is central, financial loss being of only secondary importance. Evidence to support 'the shock of retirement' thesis is remarkably limited (Minkler, 1982). Analyses of data from the Norwegian Level of Living Surveys from the latest decade do not support this thesis either (Wærness, 1983). These surveys show that most men report significant changes in their situation, mostly for the better, and report relief from the strain of work and increased leisure as the major advantages. Very few men report economic disadvantages. The majority of the elderly women report that they do not see much change in their situation when reaching the age of retirement, except that a good many report an improvement in their private economy. The improvement in private economy can be explained by housewives' entitlement to old-age pension, which means that many married women who are today of retirement age receive an income of their own for the first time in many years when they reach the age of 67. The greatest problem in everyday life is related to bad health, a minority of the pensioners reporting other problems. If we know that old people are more prone to report satisfaction, despite relatively worse living conditions than younger people, the idea that the main problem of ageing in the modern welfare state is related to the shock of retirement from working life should be re-examined and qualified. At the very least, this way of stating the problem is today more relevant to the position of middle-class men than it is either to women or to a high proportion of working-class men.

Bringing women into social gerontology implies that since women and men occupy different roles and statuses throughout their life-cycles, research on the problems of ageing and the welfare measures most suitable to relieve these problems, should take into account the assumption that older men and women also in old age may well exhibit different characteristics and behaviour. This also means that we can expect the sexes to differ with respect to what kind of help and care is less stigmatizing in different kinds of dependency situations. From this perspective, it seems reasonable to expect that the factors leading to client status in the public home-help service are different for men and women. The analyses presented in Table 6.4, based on data on the age group 65–80 from the Norwegian Level of Living Study 1980, support this assumption. Even though the proportion of the elderly receiving this service is the same for both sexes (about 10 per cent in this sample), the variables explaining why they are becoming clients are different and partly work in opposite directions. For older women, good health seems to be the most important factor in preventing client status in this service, and integration with an informal social network actually *increases* the probability of being a client. For older men, the social network variables have the opposite effect, and the health condition has less importance than for women. Oversimplifying to some extent, we might say that for older women the home-help service is primarily a health service, while for older men it is to a greater extent a social service, substituting the help and services which otherwise wives and other female family members would provide.

Qualitative studies give a more thorough understanding of the relation between public and family care for older women in the Scandinavian welfare state today (Nordhus, 1981; Widding Isaksen, 1983; Bruland Aure, 1984). Older women who as a result of physical disability no longer manage their own household work and/or personal hygiene, seem to prefer to become a client of the home-help services instead of becoming totally dependent on informal care provided by close family members. This seems valid even when they are on good terms with their family members and highly appreciate the help and care they get from them. Family care seems most valuable when they are not totally dependent on it. On the other hand they seem to define the public care services as social rights which they have as citizens in a welfare state – rights they consider should be met when they can no longer manage on their own. These studies show that there is no reason to believe that the public care system has decreased older women's efforts to manage

**Table 6.4** Discriminant analyses: The relative weight of different variables as barriers to client status in the public home-help service for women and men separately[a] (age group 65–80 years).

|  | Variables | Discriminant function | |
|---|---|---|---|
|  |  | Women | Men |
| Health variable | Age | −0.237 | −0.624 |
|  | Physical health | 0.726 | 0.456 |
|  | Mental health | 0.210 | 0.126 |
| Social network variables | Marital status | 0.093 | 0.494 |
|  | Household composition | −0.068 | 0.277 |
|  | Unpaid help from outside the household | −0.237 | 0.215 |
|  | Contact with siblings | −0.128 | 0.110 |
|  | Contact with close friends in the neighbourhood | −0.017 | 0.099 |
|  | Contact with neighbours | −0.158 | −0.039 |
|  | Children | 0.010 | −0.248 |
|  | Education | 0.093 | 0.108 |
|  | Urbanization | 0.169 | 0.211 |
|  | Canonical correlation | 0.399 | 0.405 |

[a]The table is based on Norwegian survey data (the Level of Living Study 1980, Central Bureau of Statistics). The physical and mental health variables are constructed as indices of several survey questions. A positive coefficient indicates that the variable works as a barrier to becoming a client in the home-help service, a negative that it has the opposite effect.

The larger the coefficient, the greater the effect. The canonical correlation coefficient shows that these variables explain the same variance between men and between women, but the pattern of the coefficients shows that variables have different weights and work partly in opposite directions for the two sexes (both discriminant analyses are significant on all levels).

*Source*: Norwegian Level of Living Study 1980.

on their own as long as possible. Neither has it led to a deterioration in the quality of their family relations. As the public home-help services have decreased their total need for the practical help and support they could receive from their family, they are to some extent able to realize 'intimacy at a distance' even when disabled.

As the shortage of this service during the last few years has increased in relation to demand, social workers' routines for controlling the clients' family care resources have tightened. Elderly women report that they feel this control insulting (Bruland Aure, 1984). In their view, their family relations are not the business of the social services. This can be interpreted as another indicator of the perception of the home-help service as a right of citizenship. Two surveys from a Norwegian municipality (including a town and a rural neighbourhood) in 1969 and 1981 support the assumption that the growth in the public home-help services has changed the attitudes to public care. While in 1969 only 16 per cent of the elderly (aged 70 and over) said they would prefer public to family care, the percentage in 1981 had increased to 58 per cent (Daatland, 1983). In a decade when government authorities have changed the political ideology of old age care from defining it as a clear responsibility of the state to putting greater weight on a shared responsibility between the state and 'the informal network' (Widding Isaksen, 1983), the preference of the elderly population seems to have changed in the opposite direction.

A fourth myth is that of antagonism between public and private care so that more private care means less public care and vice versa. Of course, to some extent the demand for care in one sphere is caused by the unavailability of care in the other. If there is no public provision of care for dependants, family or friends must step in; if neither private nor public care is provided, the needs of the dependants will not be met. But to think in terms of *either* private *or* public care is much too simplified. The provision of care in society is not a zero-sum activity, there is no fixed amount of care to be provided and to be divided between the public and private spheres. In fact, much more old age care is provided in today's society than one or two generations ago, both because there are more elderly people, which means that there are more people who need some form of care, and because those who depend on care, like other citizens, expect an improvement of their standard of living. Thus, even if the family had a constant capacity to provide private care, there would still be an increasing demand for public care. The need for care outgrowing the capacity of the family is probably a more powerful force behind the rapid growth of public care systems than the alleged tendency of the modern family not to find time for, or to neglect, its elderly members. Except for the minority of the elderly who are institutionalized, public old age care is most often a *supplement* to informal care, not a *substitution*. Often the public care provided is the minimum which is needed to enable the family to take the main responsibility for its old members, as for example when the family is relieved by the home-help service of some of the most demanding chores such as the cleaning and the laundry. A great many of the clients receive much less home-help service than seems reasonable after an evaluation of their need for care and of the heavy burdens the informal care puts on many female family members (Wærness, 1982; Widding Isaksen, 1983). Shortage of public care services in relation to increasing needs often leads to a greater dependence on daughters particularly. Often both mothers and daughters find such dependency relations unacceptable, suffer a great deal of emotional strain and show symptoms of mental ill-health as a consequence (Nordhus *et al.*, 1986).

The meaning of family care has, however, to some extent changed as a result of the increased labour force participation of women and the increased supply of public care. Although direct family care is still very important, indirect care in helping the elderly to acquire public care is of increasing importance. Because of bureaucratic and other problems, it is often not easy to make use of the opportunities offered by the public system. In particular elderly people often do not have the necessary skills or stamina to find out what their rights and opportunities are, or to deal with the welfare bureaucracy. According to these assumptions it might be true that the probability of acquiring *non-stigmatizing* public care is greater for those old people who have the support and help of an informal caring network, family or otherwise, than for the elderly who do not have such informal resources, but may have the same or more need for public care. We do not have complete information about the degree to which this assumption fits the facts, but we have studies based on small samples that show this to be true for some of the health and social services (Daatland and Sundstrøm, 1985; Wærness, 1982).

More community care today, in the meaning of more elderly

people becoming well integrated in informal social networks, could therefore mean that the demand for at least some of the non-stigmatizing public care services, perceived as citizens' rights, would increase rather than decrease.


## The home-help service – from the outset based on the traditional role of the housewife

Analysing the governmental reports on old age care from the period 1950–82 and the parliamentary debates connected to these reports, Widding Isaksen (1983) found that during the whole period the primary intention behind the public domiciliary care services was to save money on public budgets. The domiciliary care services were intended first and foremost to replace expensive institutional care, both by making it possible to shorten the length of stay for hospital patients and by delaying or impeding other kinds of institutional care.

Until the end of the 1960s, there was no debate as to what kind of care might be best for the individual. The welfare of the individual dependant was not until then a subject for discussion, and there was no questioning of the quality of institutional care. The main criticism of institutions was that they were too expensive.

When the ideology of community care as being both cheaper and morally preferable had become an important argument for the development of domiciliary care services, the focus of interest in governmental reports shifted from the professional home nursing services to the more amateurish home-help services. Middle-aged housewives were explicitly said to be the preferred work-force for this service on the ground that this group had unoccupied time (since they no longer had children to care for), and could work part-time (since they still had their own household work to do). Until recently it was not assumed that 'home-helper' could be an occupation in the sense that women could provide for themselves by working in this service (Widding Isaksen, 1983). As shown in Figure 6.3, the home-help services are not yet 'professionalized' in the sense of being a source of full-time employment for most of the workers. This service is heavily based on the supply of middle-aged

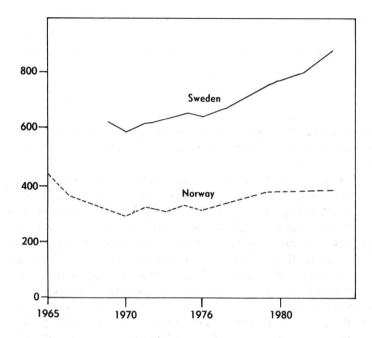

**Figure 6.3** Number of hours per year per employee in the public home-help services in Sweden and Norway, 1965–82. (*Source*: Daatland and Sundstrøm, 1985)

and elderly women who work part-time, giving flexible and versatile help to a few clients to whom they also have a personal attachment.

The organization of the service is however in the process of changing. The need for change is a consequence both of a diminishing supply of middle-aged housewives who are willing and feel able to work on the same terms as before, and also of the necessity to secure the individual home-helper the same rights as other employees. Although the social authorities recognize that the clients would prefer the kind of personal and comprehensive help most of them hitherto have had, it is at the same time admitted that it is difficult to find measures to change the organization without impersonalizing the service. As the 'reserve army' of middle-aged full-time housewives is decreasing (more rapidly in Sweden than in

Norway), it has become necessary to recruit young women (and in Sweden also some young men) to this service. This change has made it evident that the home-helpers' work is both physically and mentally demanding – often too demanding for inexperienced and unskilled young women or men.

Some special training programmes for home-helpers have been organized, more extensive in Sweden than in Norway. So far it is too early to evaluate the long-term consequences of this change. A special training programme organized by many Swedish municipalities in the 1970s was not considered to be very successful. A very high proportion of the women who had received this training said that the actual content of the job as home-helper did not correspond very well with the training and therefore they wanted other types of jobs. (Pensionarundersøkningens rapporter om social hemhalp m.m. 1979.)

Reorganization of this service in such a way that self-organized groups of home-helpers acquire the responsibility for organizing help received by groups of clients seems to solve some problems, especially for the workers, but creates or makes visible other problems, especially of providing adequate care for the most helpless clients (Wærness and Gough, 1985). Professionalizing and organizing the home-help services according to the general norms for rational behaviour in the public sphere seem, if not impossible, at least problematic. I have argued that this is partly due to 'the rationality of caring' being different from and to some degree contradictory to the 'scientific and bureaucratic rationality' on which professional authority and control in the field of reproduction is based and legitimated (Wærness, 1984a).

When, in an effort to realize the goal of community care, governmental authorities promote more family care, help from neighbours, and voluntary work, rather than developing public care services in the community, this can be seen as an implicit acknowledgement of such a contradiction. (This is not to suggest that the economic recession has not been the most important factor behind the change in policy, but it does offer an additional explanation which makes it more understandable that this new policy should so easily become accepted by all political parties.) What is not acknowledged in this new policy, in addition to it being based on the aforementioned myths, is that due both to the changing social context of the intergenerational relations in the family and to the increasing integration of women in labour market participation, informal care-giving has acquired quite a different meaning for providers on the one hand and receivers on the other.

## The changing social context of the intergenerational bond in the family

The consequences for care in old age of the change in the generational picture in Western societies during recent decades have also not been seriously discussed or analysed. The fact that we nowadays live in a multigenerational rather than a three-generational world, not only on the societal but also on the family level, has not yet been taken into account in social policy and planning.

With life expectancy of over seventy-five years for women, parents and children will have more than fifty years of overlapping life. For the majority of these years there will be adults on both sides of the intergenerational relationship. The opportunity for relationships as adults will also be increasingly common between grandparents and grandchildren. As a consequence of these phenomena, it follows that parents and children may grow old together, indeed, a growing number of mothers may outlive their sons. Thus, barring drastic changes in age differences between spouses or in mortality patterns, an increasing number of families will go through a stage of two generations of pensioners, sometimes followed by two generations of widows (Hagestad, 1981).

Families will mirror the change in age composition witnessed on the societal level; they will have steadily growing numbers surviving to old age. Some of them, mostly women, will survive to advanced old age and will, most likely, require a period of increased care. As most frail elderly men have a wife as the main carer, most often it will be old women's need for care which will bring strain to the intergenerational bonds. Since women's pensions are much lower than men's this also means a greater risk for women of becoming dependent on the younger generation.

Due to the rise of the multigenerational family, the exchange of material resources and highly practical and necessary forms of help, assistance and care between generations has become exceedingly complex, spanning several generations and multiple domains of exchange. Often it implies that the middle generation may find themselves in a stressful bridge position. They have two generations who have a claim on their resources, both material and emotional. As the most important intergenerational link in modern society seems to be that between the mother and daughter, and the caring function is primarily ascribed to women, it is most often the women 'in the middle' who have to bear the burden of maintaining their kin. The increasing divorce rate among the younger generation may add to this strain. Hagestad (1982) gives an illustrative example of this: when discussing possible current dilemmas of the middle generation, a tearful woman in the audience described her own situation: 'My 32 year divorced daughter has just moved back home — broke and depressed; my 86 year old mother has just had a stroke. I don't know if I can take it all' (p. 24). As the bulk of the helping that in Western society is reported as community care on closer scrutiny turns out to be care by close female relatives (Abrams, 1977), the lack of systematic knowledge concerning the changing demographic picture of the multigenerational family is an additional factor in rendering the new policy on community care unrealistic.

## The need for a different social policy

To develop a future-oriented social policy more related to the needs of women and the weakest members of society, we have to recognize that the welfare state is fundamentally based on the traditional division of labour between the sexes. It has not only presumed a male family head through which resources could flow and be distributed, it has also presumed a female service provider, a person able both to provide concrete services and care, and to relate to the services provided by the state and the market. We must also acknowledge that families do not only consist of parents with small children and that the integrative function of the family in an age-stratified, complex, and rapidly changing society seems import-ant in a way which hitherto has not been adequately recognized. It should also be appreciated that the existence of the welfare state is, in a number of ways, more important for women than for men. The protection of the public welfare institutions is therefore as important from a feminist point of view as it is from the point of view of redistribution or of the well-being of the recipients.

The fact that the importance of women both as clients and as employees in the welfare state services is not matched by a corresponding status as citizens and decision-makers (Hernes, 1984) may be one reason why social services tend to be planned 'from above' rather than 'from below', and why the new changes in social policy ideology are so poorly adapted to what is probably the most significant element of present change in the social structure of the Western societies: namely, the integration of women into the mainstream of society. An increased representation of women in the decision-making bodies on all levels in the welfare state is therefore *one* necessary reform for developing a social policy more fitted to the realities of today.

On a more concrete level, one key to improving the public care system in the Scandinavian countries today should lie in a far better recognition of the role and significance of informal care in the present system. The public care system's lack of recognition of the strengths of informal care often leads to offering services which are of little use to dependent clients and their families (Rønning, 1985).

Improving the co-ordination between public and informal care almost certainly implies that the trend towards a steadily increasing professionalization and specialization in the health and social services has to be broken. This means that a greater part of employees in the future have to provide more flexible, comprehensive and versatile services than most professionals are doing today.

Such a despecialization of the public care system is difficult for many practical and technical reasons, and also because it opens up deep-rooted conflicts of interests, mainly because such policies are contrary to the wishes of most of the welfare professions as expressed through their organizations. Not much more can be said here other than that it is sometimes necessary to bring conflicts of interests out in the open and to face them head on, and that although the *raison d'être* of the welfare state is to provide services for its clients, there are also conflicts of interests between those who deliver the services and those who receive and/or need them.

To make community care a realistic ideal today should imply that we first and foremost concentrate on how to reorganize and strengthen the public care system. It also should imply that we recognize the limit of this ideal. In the foreseeable future it is likely that many of the most disabled elderly will find some kind of highly organized care service on a residential basis to be the only, and sometimes even the best, alternative. Both in social policy and social research, therefore, more attention should be directed towards reducing to a minimum those specific characteristics of Goffmann's (1961) '*total institution*' that can exist in such organizations. By concentrating on basic individual rights and needs, and on the art of the possible, there should be the potential for social research to make an important contribution towards realizing this goal.

## Notes

1. The Norwegian word 'omsorg' has very much of the same connotations as the English word 'caring' or care. My own theoretical reasoning about 'omsorg', which I started in 1979, could therefore easily be translated into English.

## References

Abrams, P. (1977), 'Community care: some research problems and priorities', in *Policy and Politics*, 6:2
Ås, Dagfinn (1984), Unpublished tables
Bruland Aure, Annlaug (1984), *Eldreomsorg i et Klientperspektiv* (Bergen: Institute of Sociology, University of Bergen)
Daatland, Svein Olav (1983), 'Eldreomsorgen i en småby: De offentlige tjenester og familiens rolle', *Tidsskrift for samfunnsforskning*, 24, pp. 155–73
Daatland, Svein Olav and Sundstrøm, Gerdt (1985), *Gammel i Norden* (Stockholm)
Goffmann, Erving (1961), *Asylums* (New York: Anchor)
Graham, Hilary (1983), 'Caring; a labour of love', in Janet Finch and Dulcie Groves, *A Labour of Love* (London: Routledge and Kegan Paul)
Hagestad, G. O. (1981), 'Problems and promises in the social psychology of intergenerational relations', in Fogel *et al.* (eds.), *Aging: stability and change in the family* (New York: Academic Press)
Hagestad, G. O. (1982), 'Divorce: The ripple effect' in *Generation*, Winter, pp. 24–5

Hernes, Helga (1984), 'Women and the welfare state: The transition from private to public dependence', in Harriet Holter (ed.), *Patriarchy in a Welfare Society* (Oslo: Universitetsforlaget)

Laslett, P. (1982), 'Foreword' in M. Mitterauer and R. Sieder, *The European Family* (Oxford: Basil Blackwell)

Lingsom, Susan (1984), 'Omsorg for ektefellen', *Tidsskrift for Samfunnsforskning*, vol. 3, pp. 245–68

Lingsom, Susan (1985), 'Uformell omsorg for syke og eldre' ('Informal care of the sick and elderly'), *SØS*, no. 57 (Central Bureau of Statistics)

Minkler, M. (1982), 'Research on health effects of retirement: An uncertain legacy', in *Journal of Health and Social Behaviour*, vol. 22, pp. 117–30

Mitterauer, M. and Sieder, R. (1982), *The European Family* (Oxford: Basil Blackwell)

Nordhus, Inger Hilda (1981), *Gammel og avhengig?* Hovedfagsoppgave i psykologi (Bergen: Department of Psychology, University of Bergen)

Nordhus, Inger Hilda, Widding Isaksen, Lise and Wærness, Kari (1986), *De fleste gamle er kvinner* (Oslo: Universitetsforlaget)

Nygård, Lars (1982), *Omsorgsressursar hos nære parørende*, NIS INTEF, Report 2 (Trondheim, Norway)

Rø, Otto Christian, and co-workers (1983), *Hjemmeboende gamles liv*, SIFF, Gruppe for helsetjenesteforskning (Oslo)

Rønning, Rolf (1985), 'Hjelpeapparat uten bakkekontakt', in *Sosiologi i dag*, nos. 3–4, pp. 71–86

Rosenmayr, L. and Køckeis, E. (1965), 'Propositions for a sociological theory of ageing and the family', *International Social Science Journal*, pp. 410–26

Shanas, Ethel (1979), 'Social myth as hypothesis: The case of the family relations of the elderly' in *Gerontologist*, vol. 19, no. 1, pp. 3–9

Stearns, P. (1977), *Old Age in European Society* (London: Croom Helm)

Sundstrøm, Gerdt (1983), *Caring for the Aged in Welfare Society* (Stockholm: Studies in Social Work, Liber Førlag)

Ungerson, Clare (1983), 'Why do women care?', in Janet Finch and Dulcie Groves (eds.), *op. cit.*

Wærness, Kari (1982), *Kvinneperspektiver pa sosialpolitikken* (Oslo: Universitetsforlaget)

Wærness, Kari (1983), *'Og nva når vi blir gamle?'*, Working Paper to the RFSP-project Family and Social Policy (Bergen: Institute of Sociology, University of Bergen)

Wærness, Kari (1984a), 'The rationality of caring', in *Economic and Industrial Democracy*, vol. 5, pp. 185–211

Wærness, Kari (1984b), 'Caregiving as women's work in the welfare state' in Harriet Holter (ed.) *op. cit.*

Wærness, Kari and Gough, Ritva (1985), 'Nar kleintens selvbestemmelse og normalisering ikke strekker til', in Ivar Bleiklie, Petter Bomann-Larsen, Eierind Falkum, Thorvald Gran and Thor Øyvind Feusen (eds.), *Politikkens forvaltning* (Oslo: Universitetsforlaget)

Weber, Marianne (1975), *Max Weber: A Biography*, Harry Zahn (ed.) (New York: John Wiley)

Widding Isaksen, Lise (1983), *Grenselandsklienter*, Working Paper to the RFSP-project Family and Social Policy. Leader: Kari Wærness (Bergen: Institute of Sociology, University of Bergen)

# CHAPTER 7

# COPING WITH CARE

## Mothers in a welfare state

ARNLAUG LEIRA

## Child care: A welfare state concern?

Recent analyses of welfare states, and recent attempts to define this form of state, commonly focus either on the use of state power to secure the reproduction of the labour force and to maintain the 'non-productive' members of the population (Gough, 1979), or on the individual's right to a decent living, supported by state guarantees and public funds (Slagstad, 1981).[1] Implicit in these definitions is the assumption, previously formulated by, for example, Horkheimer (1972) and Parsons (1956), that in the modern state the family is rapidly losing most of its functions. Feminist research since the 1970s has often echoed such characterizations, for example when analysing the welfare state in terms of transfers from private to public dependency, or of the state's 'taking over' the tasks of social reproduction (Hernes, 1982; Balbo, 1987; Eisenstein, 1979).

The increasing public control of and spending on matters that used to be left to the province of the family, the church or charity unquestionably delineate central features in the history of the welfare state. Nevertheless the development of a multiplicity of welfare state provisions has not followed a single course. Institutional analyses that focus too narrowly on the activities of the state can easily under-estimate the different family strategies pursued by different welfare states, and neglect the complex and uneven development between various sectors of welfare state services. Moreover, an emphasis on the shrinking importance of the 'family' often minimizes the importance of the gender presumptions that lie behind welfare state policies, and hides the fact that 'family' policies affect women and men differently.

Even in Scandinavia, where the welfare state services are generally considered to be well developed, caring for the 'non-productive' part of the population has not by any means been completely transferred to the state. In fact, the role of the state in some fields of social reproduction is remarkably modest. Providing for the everyday welfare of the very young and the very old is still to a large extent in private hands, usually in the hands of women. The importance of sector-specific, empirical studies in an assessment of the various, sometimes contradictory processes shaping the welfare states of the 1980s comes out clearly in Scandinavian analyses (e.g. Wærness, 1982, 1984; Lingsom, 1985; Borchorst and Siim, 1983, 1987; Siim, 1984; Leira, 1983, 1987b). These analyses also argue – as is often the case in international feminist research – that it is essential to deconstruct the family into its component parts in order to allow for gender-specific analyses of welfare state policies.

Conceptualizing 'child care' as 'work', I shall in this article discuss the recent changes in the border lines between the welfare state and the family as shown in one limited but vital field of social reproduction: the provision of child care. Two processes are in focus: the modernization of motherhood introduced by the mothers who joined the formal labour market, and the collectivization of child care. By examining the mutual influence of these processes I shall outline how the relationship between the welfare state and mothers is being restructured. A shift from family to public responsibility in pre-school socialization is often pointed out in Scandinavian research (for an overview, see Leira, 1987b). My analysis shows that women's lateral self-organization has been as important as state intervention in the restructuring of child care services for mothers in employment.

The organization of everyday child care is essential to an examination of the situation of women in modern welfare states. Some feminist analyses of present-day 'patriarchy' argue that child-rearing is basic in maintaining the dominance of men, and that 'political motherhood' (the responsibility accorded to women for the primary socialization and upbringing of children) is a strong element in the subordination of women (e.g. Eisenstein, 1979). The welfare state accordingly may be seen as a transformation of the power structure within which women act, in other words a shift from private to public patriarchy. Basing my case on Norwegian data, I argue that the relationship of the welfare states to the mothers is ambivalent, shaped by contradictions as well as mutual dependence.

## 'Care' conceived as 'work'

The term 'welfare state' is used here in its commonsense meaning, as referring to a system of government provisions and legal arrangements which guarantees for the individual a minimum level of living and a certain security as regards her health and welfare. Although references are often made to the 'Scandinavian welfare states', there is no uniform Scandinavian model for reproduction policies (Leira, 1987b). Public investment in motherhood, fatherhood, and childhood differs between Denmark, Norway and Sweden, and the public share of reproduction costs varies considerably between the three countries. Unless otherwise stated, my illustrations are from Norway.

One of the prominent features of the modern welfare state is an expanded public responsibility which provides for those who cannot do so by themselves and, conversely, the prolonged periods of childhood and old age are a product of the welfare state. Childhood in the welfare state is conceived of as the period of life when the new generation of citizens is in need of nurture and care, socialization and control. In Norwegian society the management of children and childhood has generally come to be considered as an interest held in common by the state and the family. No general agreement exists, however, as to how the responsibility for early child care and education is to be divided. In many respects the provision of child care appears to be a border area of 'grey zone' where the boundaries between the state and the family – usually represented by the mother – are in the process of renegotiation.

My analysis of child care organization is done within a Scandinavian tradition in which 'care-giving' is conceptualized as 'work' (Wærness, 1982; Lingsom, 1985; Leira, 1983). The Norwegian term 'omsorg', which can be generally translated as 'care', has a dual connotation, meaning both 'caring for' and 'caring about'. According to the terminology suggested by the Norwegian sociologist Kari Wærness, 'care-giving *work*' should be distinguished from 'care', and also from 'servicing'. The term 'care-giving work' (corresponding to 'omsorgsarbeid') is reserved for the activities entailed in caring for persons who are unable to take care of themselves, for example the very young and the very old. It is not the material need to produce for survival which defines 'caring' as 'work', but the normative obligation to intervene, evoked by the need of the other. Wærness (1982, 1984) assumes that 'care-giving work' encompasses both the practical tasks embedded in 'caring for', and also the concern for the well-being of the other implied in 'caring about'. 'Care-giving work' thus has a dual normative content; the obligation to help and assist those who cannot take care of themselves, with the further provision that, in so doing, the carer should have a positive attitude towards the recipient, of respect and caring about. (For perceptive discussions of 'caring', see Ungerson, 1983; Graham, 1983. Finch (1986) gives an introduction to Norwegian feminist research on 'caring'.)

Analytically, distinctions must be made between a norm prescribing action on behalf of a person in need of care, and another prescribing acting with positive affections, and also between the act of caring and its meaning to the persons involved. Caring in everyday life is done for a variety of reasons, and certainly with mixed emotions. When 'labour outlasts love', in Hilary Graham's formulation, caring activities are still, in many cases, carried out (Noddings, 1984; Ungerson, 1987). Analysing as 'compulsory altruism' caring relationships developed within a setting of male domination and women's subordination, for example within marriage, Land and Rose (1985) question the assumption of caring as an expression of genuine affection.

In this context I will focus more on the 'labour' than on the 'love' aspects in caring. Conceptualizing 'caring' as 'work' has the obvious advantage of allowing an analysis of different forms of care-giving work in context, irrespective of the public/private distinction or forms of recompense. Without arguing that child care is necessarily all work or that only work activities matter, a common conceptual framework comprising all forms of care-giving work has proved useful in my studies where the restructuring of motherhood and child care has been in focus.

Everyday care-giving work encompasses a great variety of organizational forms. The distinctions often made between formal and informal, paid and unpaid, private and public care-giving are too simple to show the diversity of arrangements and the processes of change. More detailed information is required in order to analyse the transformations in the child care structure. My typology is based upon the institutional setting of the activity, to which is added a consideration of the types of contract or norms of reciprocity that are used to regulate the exchange (Leira, 1983). Everyday child care accordingly is carried out as follows:

1. Unpaid work within one's own household.
2. Regular employment.
3. Paid, irregular work ('shadow' or 'hidden' work, i.e., work done for pay but not reported for taxation).
4. Unpaid work exchanged within social networks, between neighbours, friends, and relatives. This unpaid work can be further subdivided according to the type of exchange involved. It may for example be done as specific exchanges, as generalized exchanges, or as one-way transfers in which no recompense is registered.

Child care is done at home, unpaid, by parents and siblings. Child care is also done by professionals, working for pay in crèches, day nurseries and nursery schools. In addition, a wide range of informal arrangements have been established, by mobilization of social support networks, reciprocity systems, and also via 'shadow' labour markets. (For a discussion of different spheres of work, see Leira and Nørve, 1977; Pahl and Wallace, 1983.) In order to examine the restructuring of care-giving in a welfare state context and to clarify the transfers of work and responsibility for the care-needing part of the population, it is necessary to differentiate analytically between the various informal institutional arrangements for care-giving. (In everyday practices the distinction between social networks and 'shadow' labour is often blurred. Network relations are 'commercialized', for example when relatives, friends and neighbours do get paid for child-minding.)

## The modernization of motherhood

In the 1970s, Norwegian society witnessed a restructuring of the labour market and the institution of the family that challenged the gendered division of labour and called for a redefinition of the accustomed boundaries between the welfare state and the family. Women played a considerable part as change agents in these processes. Entering the labour market in large numbers, they altered the composition of the labour force, expanded the idea of 'normal' work hours, challenged sexual stereotyping of jobs and pay, and demanded that employment become more compatible with parental and family responsibilities. In women's tripartite income maintenance system, where marriage and family, labour market, and social security were the main institutions (Dahl, 1984) the relative importance of the marriage contract declined, while that of the work contract and state-guaranteed economic transfers increased.

In the mid-1970s the participation rates of adult women in the United Kingdom and in Norway were fairly even, with 55.1 per cent and 53.3 per cent respectively. From 1973 to 1986 there was an increase in women's labour market participation of between 15 per cent and 20 per cent in all the Scandinavian countries, while the increase registered for Britain during the same period was 7.8 per cent. In 1986, almost 80 per cent of Danish and Swedish women were in formal employment, while Norwegian women's participation rate at 71 per cent was rapidly catching up; that of British women had grown much more slowly and in 1986 was, in comparison, relatively low at 61.0 per cent (see Table 7.1). During the 1970s and early 1980s there was a net increase in employment in Norway, constituted primarily by women, many of whom work part-time (Table 7.2). The labour market participation of men has been constant during this period; thus women's share of the labour force has grown, reaching 43 per cent in 1984, compared with 29 per cent in 1972. Women's share of unemployment has also increased during the recent economic recession, and the proportion of unemployed women in Norway has surpassed that of men, but has not yet reached 5 per cent of the female work force (Table 7.3).

Even though Norwegian women and men have become more equal with respect to formal economic activity, the gender differences in the labour market still persist, as shown for example in average weekly hours, which, in 1984, were twenty-nine hours for women and forty-one hours for men. In addition, horizontal and vertical sex segregation, more strongly pronounced in Norway than in the rest of the OECD countries (Skrede, 1984), and a certain

**Table 7.1** Women's labour force participation rate (percentages).

|  | 1973 | 1986 | percentage increase |
|---|---|---|---|
| Denmark | 61.9 | 76.5 | +14.6 |
| Norway | 50.6 | 71.0 | +20.4 |
| Sweden | 62.6 | 78.3 | +15.7 |
| UK | 53.2 | 61.0 | +7.8 |

*Source*: OECD *Employment Outlook*, September 1988, Table H.

**Table 7.2** Part-time employment in 1986.

|  | Part-time employment in 1986 as a proportion of: | | | |
|---|---|---|---|---|
|  | Total employment | Male employment | Female employment | Women's share in part time employment |
| Denmark[a] | 23.8 | 8.4 | 43.9 | 80.9 |
| Norway | 28.1 | 10.3 | 51.3 | 79.2 |
| Sweden | 23.5 | 6.0 | 42.8 | 86.6 |
| UK[a] | 21.2 | 4.2 | 44.9 | 88.5 |

[a]Data refer to 1985.
*Source*: OECD *Employment Outlook*, September 1987, p. 29.

**Table 7.3** Unemployment rates by sex, 1975, 1983, 1985.

|  | Women | | | Men | | |
|---|---|---|---|---|---|---|
|  | 1975 | 1983 | 1985 | 1975 | 1983 | 1985 |
| Denmark | 5.1 | 12.3 | 8.9 | 4.7 | 10.7 | 5.9 |
| Norway | 2.9 | 3.8 | 3.1 | 1.9 | 2.9 | 2.1 |
| Sweden | 2.1 | 3.5 | 2.9 | 1.3 | 3.4 | 2.8 |
| UK | 1.4 | 8.0 | 8.8 | 4.3 | 13.3 | 13.4 |

*Source*: OECD *Employment Outlook*, September 1987, Table L.

amount of sex discrimination in pay (Rødseth and Titlestad, 1984) mean that few women earn a 'family wage' sufficient to support themselves and their children. Gender inequalities become even more evident when waged and unwaged work are considered in context, as was done in the Norwegian time–budget analyses from 1970–81 and 1980–1. On average women work as many hours per day as men do, but women get paid for a smaller proportion of their work (Lingsom and Ellingsæter, 1983). Nevertheless, it is significant that women's economic dependence on individual men has been reduced. The long-term implications of this, for example for the division of resources and the power structure in households, remain to be seen.

The most striking feature of the Norwegian labour market of the 1970s is the rapid recruitment of married women and mothers to formal employment. In a Scandinavian context Norway appears to have been a stronghold for the gendered division of labour, ascribing the breadwinning to the men and the homemaking to the women, which is commonly interpreted as a result of its comparatively late industrialization and urbanization (see Borchorst, Chapter 8 in this volume, also Skrede, 1984; Anttalainen, 1984). The ideological support of the nuclear family may also have been more pronounced in Norway. The strength of the conventional nuclear family can be captured in census data, showing that only 5.4 per cent of Norwegian married women were registered as employed in 1950. By 1960, 9.5 per cent reported employed status. (Norwegian feminist research has documented an under-registration of married women's waged work in earlier censuses (Skrede, 1973) yet the differences between Denmark, Sweden and Norway as regards the level of married women's employment are not disputed.) For mothers to remain in employment while their children were below statutory school-age (which is seven in Norway) was unexpected and most unusual in the 1950s and 1960s. By 1980 this was what most mothers did, mainly on a part-time basis, following patterns established earlier by women in the neighbouring countries, in Western Europe, and in the United States (Amsden, 1980; OECD, 1981; Anttalainen, 1984).

The causes of the new trends in women's economic activity from the 1960s onwards have been much debated (for a review of the Scandinavian discussion see Anttalainen, 1984). An important factor in Norway was a restructuring of the demand for labour, a tightening labour market with a corresponding need to mobilize labour reserves, of which married women constituted the only segment of any size. (The alternative of encouraging rapid increase in immigration was not seriously considered.) From the late 1960s the expansion of public services in health, education and welfare made a great impact on women's job opportunities by creating jobs in local labour markets and in fields traditionally regarded as typically women's work.

Women's attitudes to the combination of wage-work and motherhood were also in the process of transformation. Answering survey questions in the 1960s and 1970s, women voiced their opinion, stating that they wanted to work for pay. A wish for money of one's own and a need to escape from the isolation of a life at home were the reasons most commonly given by those who wanted a change (SSB, 1968). Though the women's response hardly carried the force of Ibsen's Nora Helmer in *A Doll's House* almost a hundred years earlier (which the pre-coded questionnaire would not allow for anyway), indirectly the answers illuminated the sadder aspects of 'situation housewife'. Public debate was divided on the issue of mothers in employment, but it was not at all unusual in the early 1970s to encounter the opinion that a mother's place was in the home.

Questions concerning mothers in employment were also raised in social research. In the influential analysis *Women's Two Roles: Work and home*', Myrdal and Klein (1957) outlined the emerging structures in the labour market participation of women, and strongly supported the view that married women be given the opportunity to join formal employment, notably in the phases of life when mothering and nurturing obligations were less demanding. The title of the book indicated, however, that the authors accepted a split in women's roles, as distinct from those of men, and accepted, too, a lack of balance in parental obligations to offspring. This view, though widespread, was not unanimously accepted at the time. The assumption that biological motherhood was necessarily tied to the menial tasks of housework was contested. The additional responsibility for children's welfare implicitly allocated to women was also questioned, and it was argued that caring for children was a moral challenge for all human beings, and a human activity not by necessity linked with women's capacity for procreation.

During the last ten to fifteen years opposition to the employment

**Table 7.4** Percentage of married mothers in employment in Norway in 1976, 1980 and 1985, by age of youngest child.

|      | All married women with children | Age of youngest child | | | |
|------|------|------|------|------|------|
|      |      | 0–2 | 3–6 | 7–10 | 11–15 |
| 1976 | 53 | 40 | 48 | 64 | 67 |
| 1980 | 62 | 48 | 58 | 71 | 75 |
| 1985 | 71 | 55 | 70 | 75 | 81 |

*Source*: Ellingsæter, 1987.

of married women has declined, influenced by the reality of women's economic activity, by the activities of the Women's Liberation Movement, and by government policies promoting equal status between women and men. The persistent sex-segregation in jobs may also have contributed to the modification of general attitudes, as it became clearly evident that women did not seriously challenge men's position in the labour market. The most dramatic consequences of women going out to work for pay were seen in families with children. Even in the families where the children were very young the dual-earner family became the norm. In the early 1980s almost 30 per cent of the 1.8 million persons in the labour force were parents of children under ten. Two out of three families with such young children were dual-earner families.

Table 7.4 shows the labour force participation of mothers, 1976–85. During this time, the mothers of children under 3 increased their participation rate from 40 per cent to 56 per cent, and the mothers whose youngest child was between 3 and 6 years old increased their employment rate from 48 per cent to 70 per cent. There was also an increase in the proportion of mothers who were in full-time employment. By 1985 approximately one in three of the employed mothers whose youngest child was under 11 years old, was in full-time waged work, i.e., thirty-five hours or more per week. The mothers having children under 3 worked full-time as often as those whose children were older.

The level of economic activity among Norwegian mothers appears to be higher than that of mothers in the United Kingdom, where 27 per cent of those with children under 5 and 64 per cent of mothers whose youngest child was between 6 and 10 were registered in employment in 1980 (Martin and Roberts, 1984). The rate of Norwegian mothers' formal employment still lags behind that of the Danish and Swedish mothers, among whom more than 80 per cent of those with children up to 6 years old are in the labour market (Leira, 1987b).

The formally employed mothers of the 1970s represented a modernization of women's role in society. A modernization of child care was also introduced when the Act governing Day Care was passed in 1975, incorporating the provision of day care into Norwegian welfare state services to the population. A connection is generally assumed to exist between these processes, the mass entry of mothers into the labour market and the public provision of day care. In Denmark and Sweden the combination of employment and motherhood was facilitated by large-scale public investments in day care (Borchorst and Siim, 1983; Näsman *et al.*, 1983). In Norway where the development was different, the public provision of child care services seems to have played a minor part in furthering the employment of mothers (Leira, 1985).

## The collectivization of child care

These dramatic increases in the labour market participation of mothers and the accompanying changes in the family caused a revival of the debate about the organization of social reproduction, caring responsibilities, and the management of everyday life. While much of the academic discussion in Britain was focused on the domestic division of labour in general (Barrett, 1980; Molyneux, 1979), a specific interest in the organization of everyday care-giving work was perhaps more characteristic of the Scandinavian approach (Leira, 1981; Finch, 1986). Questions concerning child care were also put on the Norwegian political agenda, raising discussion about the boundaries between the welfare state and the family in pre-school socialization.

State intervention, at least in some family matters, seems to have been more easily accepted in Norway than in the United Kingdom (cf. Land, 1979) as witnessed for example by the establishment of a

## 144    *Arnlaug Leira*

Norwegian Ministry of Family and Consumer Affairs in 1956
(although later this Ministry was merged with another and became
the Ministry of Consumer Affairs and Government Administration). However, the conflicting demands of labour market organization and family obligations, of production and generational reproduction were not immediately conceived of as being a matter for
public concern. In some of the larger cities the city council provided
day care facilities, but it was not until 1975 that the provision of day
care was incorporated into national family policy with the passing of
'Lov om barnehager' (Act governing Day Care), from which the
idea of public day care as 'mass consumption' has developed. In
1975 public day care (referring to day care approved and subsidized
by the state) accommodated only 7 per cent of pre-school children.[2]
A decade later, 27 per cent of pre-school children were attending
state-sponsored day care. Coverage is best for the older children,
but very modest for children aged 0–2 (see Figure 7.1 and Table
7.5). Only about half the places in public day care accept children
for thirty-one hours or more per week (1985), which means that a
considerable proportion of the services offered are not aimed at
meeting wage-working parents' demand for competent child care to
cover a full working day.

   Although the Day Care Act was important in the reconstitution
of public and private responsibilities in child care, the state-
sponsored day care system was not of great significance in promoting the development of the dual-income family. State intervention
came too late and expanded too slowly for that. When the law was
passed, these families numbered more than one-third of the
households with young children. According to the Family Ministry's estimates only a minority of children from dual-earner families
had access to state-supervised day care at that time. In the decade
following the passing of the Day Care Act government policies were
not expanded so as to comply with the child care needs of parents in
employment. While the supply of public day care increased,
demand also grew to the extent that by the early 1980s approximately 70–5 per cent of the children of dual-earner families were *not*
being cared for in public day care facilities. According to Table 7.5,
it is evident that the majority of working mothers of children under
3 years old still do not have access to the public day care system. For
older children more places are available, but a sizeable proportion
will not gain access to the public day care services.

Per cent

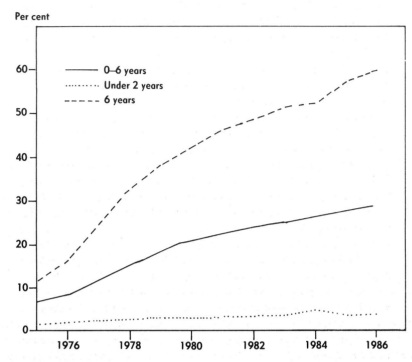

**Figure 7.1** Children in public day care in Norway, by age, as percentage of all children in the age group, 1975–86. (*Source*: Kindergartens and leisure time centres 1986, NOS B 722, Central Bureau of Statistics, Oslo 1987)

**Table 7.5** The percentage of children in Norway aged 0–6 attending state-sponsored day care by age, 1981 and 1984.

|      | Age of children | | | |
|------|------|------|------|------|
|      | 0–6  | 0–2  | 3–4  | 5–6  |
| 1981 | 23   | 6    | 27   | 43   |
| 1984 | 26   | 7    | 32   | 49   |

*Source*: Leira, 1987.

With the passing of the Day Care Act, state intervention in pre-school education was accepted by all political parties as a matter of principle. The relationship between the welfare state and the family was redefined, so as to augment the responsibility of the state and the public spending in this field of social reproduction. Public day care, developed by professionals, was to integrate and give equal importance to caring and education. As stated by Stortinget (the Norwegian Parliament), the long-term aim of government policy was to make public day care available to all children whose parents wished for it. Contrary to the principles of the school system, the Act did not establish day care as a universal service free of charge, as a benefit to which all children were entitled. The provision of day care was largely left to the local authorities and national aims for the expansion of child care services have proved hard to fulfil.

The Act governing Day Care introduced concepts about childhood, motherhood and everyday family life that were remarkably easily accepted, at least among parents with young children, considering that collective day care was a completely new experience to most families when the law was passed. Attending high-quality, state-supervised day care soon became established as a norm for good pre-school socialization, which in turn, of course, contributed to an increase in the demand. Through the 1970s and early 1980s the gap between supply and demand has been a constant characteristic of child care organization. This gap is largely generated by the welfare state, which in its expansion offered jobs to Norwegian mothers, thus contributing much to the increase in demand for day care. Welfare state employment policies, however, operated on the assumption of free and mobile labour, and did not incorporate measures to meet the care-giving responsibilities of the work-force. A considerable proportion of the cost of generational reproduction, as expressed in the provision of child care, remains a family concern. In retrospect family policies seemed to be shaped more by a presumption of a permanent home-making mother than by the considerable transformations in family life brought about by mothers going out to work for pay.

Gradually other reforms were carried through that gave some concessions to the child care commitment of employed parents, as witnessed by 'Arbeidsmiljølova' (the Work Environment Act) of 1977, which specified certain rights for parents in connection with caring for young children. The entitlement obtained by salaried parents to various leaves of absence is evidence of something rarely seen in our society, that the needs of social reproduction are given priority when they conflict with the demands of production. In 1987 maternity leave was expanded to twenty-two weeks, with wage compensation, and fathers got the right to take unpaid leave of absence for two weeks in connection with the birth of a child. The right to unpaid parental leave during the child's first year of life which may be split between the parents was also granted, though reasons of economy obviously may limit its use. Moreover, parents are entitled to leave of absence for ten days each per year, and single parents for twenty days when a child under eleven, or her minder, is ill. This law-making is interesting because it signals that labour market organization is having to make some accommodation to the reproduction of generations. The intervention was restricted, however, to extraordinary needs for care, stemming from relatively rare events in the employed parents' lives. It was not considered necessary to include the everyday requirements for child care in the Act.

## Child care and employment: coping strategies

When Norwegian mothers were recruited into the labour market in large numbers the question of who should mind the children had not been solved. In the market, the labour of mothers was 'collectivized' to an extent not matched by the provision of collective day care. As in many other Western European countries, the politics of production and reproduction were not synchronized (for an overview, see Pichault, 1984). It comes as no surprise, therefore, that Norwegian families in which both parents go out to work often report difficulties in bridging the gap between two incompatible work organizations, that of the labour market and that of the home. Similar difficulties are clearly brought out in a survey carried out in the Common Market countries, in which it is stated that in dual-earner families 'the problem of arrangements for looking after the children is by far the most preoccupying, ahead of the problems of housing, [and] money' ('The Europeans and their children', quoted in Pichault, 1984, p. 10).

*Arnlaug Leira*

Basically the reduction of maternal time-resources available for child care could be compensated in two ways: either by an internal reorganization in the family, allocating more of the fathers' and older siblings' time to care for young children; or by providing supplementary resources from outside. According to the Norwegian time–budget analyses and labour market statistics, the average husband bears a very modest burden of domestic labour in all types of households, even in those where the woman has a full-time contract in waged work. There is no indication of fathers replacing mothers as home-makers. A reversal of 'parental roles' is not common. The growth in employment of mothers seems to have made a very moderate impact on the average father's use of time at work and in the home. In housework and child care what Morgan (1975) has called a 'generalized lack of reciprocity between the sexes', is still striking.

In 1980–1 the fathers of pre-school children spent more time on domestic work and child care than fathers ten years earlier. However, in these families the mothers spent more than double the number of hours that fathers spent on housework and child care (Lingsom and Ellingsæter, 1983). An interesting recent study of children's work hypothesizes that children aged 10–12 may represent more important child care assets in dual-earner families than the average father does (Solberg and Vestby, 1987).

During the 1970s, mothers were changing their patterns of daily life and experimenting with various combinations of motherhood and employment. The everyday behaviour of the average fathers did not change to the same extent, indicating perhaps that they had more to lose in the process, or that there was less leeway for experiments in the male role structure. Surveys of child care organization present some forms of household in which the fathers do play a more prominent part in caring for the children, but these are comparatively few and far between (see Leira, 1985, for a review). In the majority of cases the mothers joined the labour market without waiting for their husbands to provide replacement in child care.

Let us look more closely at the coping strategies of dual-earner families: in the early 1980s approximately one in four of pre-school children from dual-earner families were admitted to public day care. The rest were cared for in private informal arrangements, or by the parents. The 1980 Level of Living Study found that an amazing 45 per cent of families where both parents were in full-time employment did not report the use of any form of extra-familial day care at all, neither private nor public, for children aged up to 9 (Hansen and Andersen, 1984). Everyday coping practices in such families indicate complex, sometimes strenuous or fragile time schedules. For example, in some families the mothers – rarely the fathers – take the children with them to work (Opdahl, 1984; Leira, 1985), and some families adjust to the use of 'parent shifts' (Kalleberg, 1983), which means fitting in their jobs at different hours so that one parent is always available to mind the children.

It is not really known whether the different solutions arise out of necessity or choice. Obviously the public day care system favours families with wage-work during the day-time. The many day care centres offering part-time attendance only is not well-suited to meet the demands of full-time working parents. For parents working shifts in industry, in hospitals or in transportation, and for those working at 'inconvenient hours', parent shift may be the only solution. We do not know, on any systematic basis, what kinds of jobs those mothers have who take their children with them to work; it is said to occur among cleaning personnel and among self-employed women in comparatively small-business firms.

Surveys done in Denmark, Norway and Sweden report inequalities in access to public day care, referring to the distribution of available places between children of different socio-economic background. The distribution appears to favour children from resourceful families more than those coming from families with comparatively few resources. Such differences in 'consumption patterns' are partly related to the regional differences in level of supply. Hours of opening and cost of places may also prevent some families from using the services offered locally. Furthermore, differences in use of the public day care services may stem from socio-cultural differences in attitudes to the forms of day care available. The local allocation procedures and criteria for priority may also contribute to a socially 'skewed' distribution. In regions where demand exceeds supply children who may all belong to highly prioritized categories will compete for the places available. What is locally considered as the 'best' or most justified distribution does not necessarily produce a similar result nationally, when the results of all local decisions are aggregated. The importance attributed to local autonomy in decisions concerning day care contributes to the national consumption patterns which in turn raises questions about distributive justice. To a large extent the problems with 'distributive justice' in day care stems from a general shortage of places, and from establishing local autonomy as a dominant principle of day care provision and distribution. It is generally acknowledged that an expansion of services is necessary in order to ensure more equitable access. All through the 1970s when the proportion of dual-income families was increasing, such families were to a large extent dependent on private, informal arrangements for child care. If the most recent survey data from the early 1980s (Hansen and Andersen, 1984; Bogen, 1987) give a fairly accurate picture of the situation, private child care arrangements have remained a cornerstone in the dual-earner family's everyday coping strategies, since more of the children from these families are minded privately than in public facilities.

## Mothers, minders, markets

The development of welfare state services to mothers may, it has been shown, break down existing informal structures that provide help and support (Lewis, 1980). This was not what happened in Norway when public investments in child care increased. The data, admittedly scarce, on the entire range of child care arrangements, not only from Norway, but also from the United Kingdom (Martin and Roberts, 1984) and the EC countries (Pichault, 1984), indicate that the use of informal resources is still important in 'generational reproduction', especially when the children are young.

When the Norwegian Day Care Act was passed two types of extra-familial day care structures were in operation. One was run by professional pre-school teachers and subsidized by public means, but could accommodate only a minority of children from dual-earner families. The other one, all private, was constituted by social network relations and 'shadow' labour. Traditional forms of child care were being merged with new ones, in arrangements that mostly involved 'non-professional' child-minders. In principle the Act might have been expanded to encompass all forms of child care provided by someone not a member of family, household or kin. No system of licensing private child-minding was established.[3] Neither was any effort made to supervise or control the informal child care markets, or to integrate the operations of the two child care structures. It was assumed that the provision of high-quality public day care would render the informal services superfluous. However, welfare state day care facilities were not developed so as to meet demand, and the formal market did not produce the services at prices which most people could afford. In this institutional impasse the families – usually the mothers – have shaped their own everyday strategies.

Private, informal arrangements for child care are organized as transfers between households, sometimes depending upon local support networks or extended reciprocity systems. Private services also depend on the mobilization of resources via informal or 'shadow' labour markets. Grandmothers and other kin, neighbours and friends are used for child care, as are au-pairs and unregistered child-minders.

Socio-cultural traditions influence parents' attitudes to extra-familial child care, and also their preferences for different forms of care. A European study indicates that attitudes to child-minding vary markedly by country, and that a considerable proportion of parents in some countries express preference for child-minders over day care centres when the children are under 3 (Pichault, 1984). Similar results are reported in a recent Norwegian study (Bogen, 1987). Whatever the preferences of Norwegian parents may be, however, their choice remains limited. Finding a private child-minder is in many cases the only option if the employment of both parents is to be maintained.

A preference for private arrangements is perhaps not only a result of a no-choice situation. Inherent in the well-functioning networks and in women's informal production of social services are principles such as self-organization, reciprocity and mutual aid, that may carry an implicit critique of the professionalism and bureaucrat-ization of the formal welfare state services. I do not perceive this criticism as supporting conservative arguments in favour of repriva-tization and minimizing of the welfare state obligations, but rather as a challenge to the present-day functioning of the welfare state services, and – to some extent – as an experimentation with alternative models for 'welfare production'.

In scenarios outlining the organization of future social services, the possibility of mutuality, reciprocal exchanges and local self-reliance replacing the distant, hierarchical services of today, is being debated (see, e.g., Lagergren *et al.*, 1982). For this to become a reality, a thorough redefinition of the boundaries between public and private responsibility is needed, as well as an examination of the part to be played by the state in social reproduction. From a woman's point of view the basic question is whether it is possible to envisage a reshaping of welfare state services in a way that furthers a co-operation with and a sustaining of informal social networks, extended support systems and reciprocity – without a perpetuation of the gendered division of work.

In Britain the problematic aspects of private child-minding have, until recently, been given more attention in social research and public debate than in Norway (Mayall and Petrie, 1977; Jackson, 1979; Bryant, Harris and Newton, 1980; Shinman, 1981). Without underestimating the problems associated with private child-minding I shall in this context focus on other aspects that also tend to be neglected in public debate: namely the importance of women's 'informal economy' in everyday care-giving practices.

According to Norwegian data, women, acting as mothers and minders, are the central agents in the shaping of an informal infra-structure in child care. More women are involved in private child care arrangements than in the public day care system. The work patterns and time schedules of mothers and minders are interlocked in the informal arrangements for child care. Mothers create for themselves a certain amount of 'spare' time, free from children that can be invested in regular employment. Minders create for themselves an opportunity to generate income, which may be more attractive than other possibilities, if alternatives exist at all. A high level of regular employment among mothers combined with a shortage of public day care provisions has mobilized labour reserves among other groups of women who are willing to mind children on a private basis. The development of the modern Norwegian dual-earner family in the 1970s has depended considerably on the conservation of a more traditional family form, in which the women retained the home-maker's role, perhaps not exclusively, but to a decisive extent. Through the organization of child care, employment-oriented and home-making women have become mutually interdependent (Leira, 1987a).

The organization of everyday 'reproduction politics' illustrates a point made by the Norwegian political scientist Helga Hernes (1984), who notes that in situations of cross-pressure women have the possibility of forming alliances with several partners, the most important being the state, men or other women. In order to combine motherhood and salaried work, women have used all these strategies. In this process, in the organization of daily child care, co-operation with other women has until now been a greater resource than the efforts of the state, and it has meant more than the fathers' contribution. The use of informal arrangements for child care supports and maintains the formal employment of mothers. Furthermore, underemployment and unemployment among other groups of women is absorbed. Thus the competition for jobs is reduced, and the shortage of regular salaried work becomes less visible. In a labour market perspective formal and informal employment are mutually dependent.

Looking at informal child care arrangements in this way presents an interpretation of the way women act which contrasts with that which is commonly characterized as women's 'self-supporting networks' or as 'informal community care', terms that tend to minimize the importance of women's work and time commitments in the development and maintenance of informal service systems. Conceptualizing informal care-giving as 'work' prevents the marginalization of women's efforts in the informal production of socially useful and necessary services. The imaginative use of social networks and of 'shadow' labour also offers interesting evidence of everyday management and gives fascinating insights into the development of systems of reciprocity and of women's coping strategies (Leira, 1983). However, the ambiguities implicit in the so-called well-functioning networks need examination and specification. For whom are they functioning well? Under what conditions? As seen from a woman's point of view they are not unambiguously 'good'. Although informal care-giving may be emotionally rewarding, and individual motivations for care-giving work are important, it is nevertheless essential not to neglect the analysis of the economic and social processes that produce an informal economy of child care, shouldered by women.

## Caring in the welfare state – caring for the welfare state?

In studies of the care-giving work carried out in the context of one modern welfare state like Norway, the importance of gender as a governing principle in the distribution of this type of work cannot be overlooked. In all forms of care-giving work women represent the majority of care-givers. This holds true whether the work is paid or unpaid, formally or informally organized. In family-based care-giving work the surplus work done by women compared with men attains considerable dimensions (Wærness, 1982). Women far outnumber men as producers of welfare state services, and represent a sizeable proportion of the 'new' working-class. Within the informal or 'shadow' labour market of care-giving, the available evidence strongly indicates that women are the predominant category of workers.

The gendered division of labour in care-giving is certainly not news. Nevertheless, its persistence deserves consideration. Even in modern welfare states, where social reproduction is taken out of the private sphere and conceived of as part of the state's sphere of influence and responsibility, the gender-typing of care-giving work is remarkable. Providing for the care-needing parts of the population may well be regarded as a sector in which the welfare state and women play the leading parts. Interpretations concerning the character of the relationship between the two differ, however. In international feminist research the assignment of caring to women is often assumed to contribute considerably to women's structurally inferior situation in society (e.g. Eisenstein, 1979). On the other hand, Scandinavian research commonly analyses the relationship as one of mutual dependence (e.g. Hernes, 1982, 1984; Borchorst and Siim, 1987; Siim, 1984). Hernes (1982) points out the possibility of alliances being formed between women and the welfare state. Borchorst and Siim (1987) argue that a partnership has developed between Danish women and the welfare state, in which the state acknowledges the dual obligations of mothers to wage-work and child care. In the political history of Norwegian 'reproduction policies' I find no evidence of such a partnership. Considering the situation of employed mothers in the Norwegian welfare state, and analysing in context the maternity benefits, parental leave, and provision of day care services, I find the relationship to be one of ambivalence and contradictions, as well as one of interdependence.

The development of formal welfare state caring supported Norwegian women's earning opportunities, reduced the dependence on individual men and strengthened the mutual dependence between the women and the state. The welfare state came to depend on the labour of women in the provision of social services. Thus women's strategic situation in society – and *vis à vis* the state – was improved. However, this was only one aspect of the relationship. The 'revolution of rising expectations' also meant increasing popular demands for welfare state services that came to be regarded as rights (Marshall, 1965), demands that could not be met within the welfare state economy. In order to provide the socially useful and necessary services needed to secure the welfare of the care-needing parts of the population, the welfare state has also had to depend on the activity of the family, usually the women, and on an informal infrastructure of services. Thus the pressure on the formal service system is reduced. Problems concerning the legitimacy of the welfare state that may easily arise when demand for necessary social services are not met, are kept at bay.

In child care, a fundamental part of social reproduction, the informal economy constituted by mothers and minders is an essential ingredient. This informal economy fills the lacunae of welfare state services, contributes to individual welfare, and maintains a general level of welfare provision and socially necessary and useful services at a minimum of costs to the welfare state economy. The costs of planning, producing and maintaining the informal services are met by mothers and minders, who supplement or make substitutes for the shortages of the state-sponsored services. Individually, the informal provisions are temporary, planned for relatively short periods of time. When analysed in the context of welfare state strategies, the use of informal services appears a fairly permanent feature. Mothers and minders function as a buffer zone, protecting the interests of the state. The expanding Norwegian welfare state upheld the gendered division of labour in the public domain and in the private sphere, and may even have strengthened it. More or less tacitly it was assumed that women would go on coping with care. In child care, as we have seen, 'political motherhood' prevailed as a basic structural element.

The contradictions in welfare state relations to mothers are also witnessed in the widespread use of unpaid and informal labour for child-minding. The welfare state did not challenge the hierarchy of work forms inherited from industrial capitalism. Rather the hierarchy was elaborated and perpetuated in the welfare state, where a series of benefits and services is not universally available, but reserved for those in formal employment only. As long as essential citizens' rights, like certain social security benefits, employment-related benefits, and access to certain types of social services, presuppose participation in formal employment, doing unpaid and informal care-giving work will imply considerable long-term costs for women.

## Notes

1. I am grateful for the helpful comments of Joan Acker, Helga Maria Hernes and Clare Ungerson on an earlier version of this paper. Parts of the chapter also appear in my report 'Models of Motherhood' (Oslo: Institute for Social Research) which was published in July 1989.
2. Day care may be provided by local authorities or by voluntary organizations, parents' co-operatives and other private bodies. In Norway approximately 40 per cent of the day care centres are established by private bodies, but authorized and subsidized by the state, and often supported economically by the local authorities as well. (Registration requirements are specified in Note 3.)
3. Some few child-minders are employed by local authorities and work in state-sponsored family day care. From 1983 private child care arrangements are required to register for approval provided:
   (a) that children attend more than twenty hours per week;
   (b) that there are more than ten children aged 3–6 present at a time, or more than five children aged under 3; and
   (c) that the child care is paid for.

## References

Amsden, A. H. (1980), 'Introduction', in A. H. Amsden (ed.), *The Economics of Women and Work* (Harmondsworth: Penguin Books Ltd)

Anttalainen, M. L. (1984), *Rapport om den könsuppdelade arbetsmarknaden* (Oslo: Nordisk Ministerråd)

Balbo, L. (1987), 'Crazy Quilts: Rethinking work and society from a woman's perspective' in A. S. Sassoon (ed.) *Women and the State* (London: Hutchinson)

Barrett, M. (1980), *Women's Oppression Today* (London: Verso Editions)

Bogen, H. (1987), *Barnepass-drøm og virkelighet* (Oslo: FAFO, rapport nr. RA: 87)

Borchorst, A. and Siim, B. (1983), *The Danish Welfare State. A Case for a Strong Social Patriarchy* (Aalborg: Universitetsforlag)

Borchorst, A. and Siim, B. (1987), 'Women and the advanced welfare state: a new kind of patriarchal power?', in A. S. Sassoon (ed.), *Women and the State* (London: Hutchinson)

Bryant, B., Harris, M. and Newton, B. (1980), *Children and Minders* (London: Grant McIntyre)

Dahl, T. S. (1984), 'Women's right to money', in H. Holter (ed.), *Patriarchy in a Welfare Society* (Oslo: Universitetsforlaget)

Eisenstein, Z. (ed.) (1979), *Capitalist Patriarchy and the Case for Socialist Feminism* (New York: Monthly Review Press)

Ellingsæter, A. L. (1987), 'Ulikhet i arbeidstidsmønstre', in *NOU* 1987:9B (Oslo)

Finch, J. (1986), 'Lessons from Norway: Women in a welfare society', *Critical Social Policy*

Frønes, I. (1985), *Barn og tilsynsordninger* (Oslo: INAS)

Gough, I. (1979), *The Political Economy of the Welfare State* (London: Macmillan Press)

Graham, H. (1983), 'Caring: A Labour of Love', in J. Finch and D. Groves (eds.), *A Labour of Love* (London: Routledge and Kegan Paul)

Hansen, A. and Andersen, A. S. (1984), *Barns levekår*, Statistiske analyser 53 (Oslo – Kongsvinger: Statistisk Sentralbyrå)

Hernes, H. (1982), *Staten – kvinner ingen adgang* (Oslo: Universitetsforlaget)

Hernes, H. (1984), 'Women and the welfare state: the transition from private to public dependence', in H. Holter (ed.), *Patriarchy in a Welfare Society* (Oslo: Universitetsforlaget)

Horkheimer, M. (1972) 'Autorität und Familie' (1936), translated as 'Authority and the family', *Critical Theory* (New York: Continuum Publishing)

Jackson, B. and Jackson, S. (1979), *Childminder: A study in action research* (London: Routledge and Kegan Paul)

Kalleberg, A. (1983), 'Foreldreskrift og kjønnsrolleforandringer', in C. Wadel (ed.), *Dagliglivets organisering* (Oslo: Universitetsforlaget)

'Kindergartens and leisure time centres 1986' (1987), NOS B 722 (Oslo: Central Bureau of Statistics)

Lagergren, M., Lundh, L., Orhan, M. and Sanne, C. (eds.) (1982), *Tid för omsorg* (Stockholm: Liber Förlag)

Land, H. (1979), 'The boundaries between the state and the family', in C. Harris (ed.), *The Sociology of the Family: New Directions for Britain* (Sociology Review Monograph, 28, University of Keele)

Land, H. and Rose, H. (1985), 'Compulsory altruism for some or an altruistic society for all', in P. Bean, J. Ferris and D. K. Whynes (eds.), *In Defence of Welfare* (London: Tavistock)

Leira, A. (1981), 'Kvinneperspektiv på arbeidssosiologien', *Tidsskrift for samfunnsforskning*, vol. 21

Leira, A. (1983), 'Kvinners organisering av dagliglivet', in C. Wadel (ed.), *Dagliglivets organisering* (Oslo: Universitetsforlaget)

Leira, A. (1985), *Regelmessig barnetilsyn*, Working Paper 4/85 (Oslo: Institute for Social Research)

Leira, A. (1987a), 'Time for work, time for care', in J. Brannen and G. Wilson (eds.), *Give and Take in Families* (London: Allen & Unwin)

Leira, A. (1987b), *Day Care in Denmark, Norway and Sweden*, Research Report 5/87 (Oslo: Institute for Social Research)

Leira, A. and Nørve, S. (1977),'Det skjulte markedet', *Tidsskrift for samfunnsforskning*, vol. 18

Lewis, J. (1980), *The Politics of Motherhood* (London: Croom Helm)

Lingsom, S. (1985), *Uformell omsorg for syke og eldre*, SØS 57 (Oslo – Kongsvinger: Statistisk Sentralbyrå)

Lingsom, S. and Ellingsæter, A. L. (1983), *Arbeid, fritid og samvær* (Oslo – Kongsvinger: Statistisk Sentralbyrå)

Lov om barnehager av 5. juni, 1975 (Day Care Act, 5 June 1975)

Lov om arbeidervern og arbeidsmiljo av 1. juli, 1977 (Act governing the Protection of Workers and Work Environment, 1 July 1977)

Marshall, T. H. (1965), *Social Policy* (London: Hutchinson)

Martin, J. and Roberts, C. (1984), *Women and Employment: A Lifetime Perspective* (London: HMSO)

Mayall, B. and Petrie, P. (1977), *Minder, Mother and Child* (London: Heinemann)

Molyneux, M. (1979), 'Beyond the domestic labour debate', *New Left Review*, 116

Morgan, D. (1975), *Social Theory and the Family* (London: Routledge and Kegan Paul)

Myrdal, A. and Klein, V. (1957), *Women's Two Roles: Work and home* (London: Routledge and Kegan Paul)

Näsman, E., Nordstrøm, K., Hammarström, R., et al. (1983), *Föräldrars arbete och barns villkor* (Stockholm: Libertryck)

Noddings, N. (1984), *Caring: A Feminine Approach to Ethics & Moral Education* (London: University of California Press)

Opdahl, S. (1984), *Aleneforeldres tidsbruk og levekår*, Rapporter 84/16 (Oslo – Kongsvinger: Statistisk Sentralbyrå)

Organisation for Economic Co-operation and Development (OECD), (1981), *Women and Employment* (Paris: OECD)

Organisation for Economic Co-operation and Development (OECD), (1988), *Employment Outlook* (Paris: OECD)

Pahl, R. E. (1980), 'Employment, work and the domestic division of labour', *International Journal of Urban and Regional Research*, vol. 4, pp. 1–19

Pahl, R. E. and Gershuny, J. I. (1979/80), 'Work outside employment: Some preliminary speculations', *New Universities Quarterly* 34

Pahl, R. E. and Wallace, C. (1983), *Household Work Strategies in Economic Recession* (Isle of Sheppey Research Studies: University of Kent at Canterbury)

Parsons, T. (1956), 'The American family: Its relations to personality and to the social structure', in T. Parsons and R. F. Bales (eds.), *Family, Socialization and Interaction Process* (Glencoe, Illinois: The Free Press)

Pichault, C. (1984), *Day-Care Facilities and Services for Children under the Age of Three in the European Community* (Luxembourg Office for Official Publications of the European Communities)

Rødseth, A. and Titlestad, K. D. (1984), 'Lønnsforskjeller mellom kvinner og menn', in T. Rødseth and K. D. Titlestad (eds.), *Kvinner i arbeid* (Oslo: Universitetsforlaget)

Shinman, S. M. (1981), *A Chance for Every Child* (London: Tavistock Publications)

Siim, B. (1984), *Women and the Welfare State – Between Private and Public Dependence*, paper presented at the Center for Research on Women, Stanford University

Skrede, K. (1973), *Sosial bakgrunn og oppvekstforhold* (INAS, notat no. 5, Oslo)

Skrede, K. (1984), *Occupational and Industrial Distribution in the ECE Region*, paper prepared for the Economic Commission for Europe

Slagstad, R. (1981), 'Velferdstaten' in *Pax Leksikon*, vol. 6 (Oslo: Pax Forlag)

Solberg, A. and Vestby, G. M. (1987), *Barnas arbeidsliv* (Oslo: NIBR)

Statistisk Sentralbyrå (SSB) (1968), *Ønsker om og behov for sysselsetting blant gifte kvinner* (Oslo: SSB)

Strømsheim, G. (1983), 'Den sårbare likestillingen' in C. Wade (ed.) *Dagliglivets organisering* (Oslo: Universitetsforlaget)

Ungerson, C. (1983), 'Why do women care?', in J. Finch and D. Groves (eds.), *A Labour of Love* (London: Routledge and Kegan Paul)

Ungerson, C. (1987), *Policy is Personal. Sex, Gender and Informal Care* (London: Tavistock)

Wærness, K. (1982), *Kvinneperspektiver på sosialpolitikken* (Oslo: Universitetsforlaget)

Wærness, K. (1984), 'Caring as Women's Work in the Welfare State', in H. Holter (ed.) *Patriarchy in a Welfare Society* (Oslo: Universitetsforlaget)

# CHAPTER 8

# POLITICAL MOTHERHOOD AND CHILD CARE POLICIES

A comparative approach to Britain and Scandinavia

ANETTE BORCHORST

## Introduction

Motherhood plays a crucial role in the lives of women and shapes their experiences fundamentally. Little girls are socialized to become mothers and they learn to be aware of human needs and take care of dependent persons. It is still widely accepted that motherhood is a very important element of female identity, if not *the* true meaning of womanhood. As a result women who do not have children often question their very identity. However, women who have children often experience it as heaven and hell at the same time. They are often trapped in contradictions between mothering and other kinds of activity outside the family.[1] Thus the conditions of 'real' mothering starkly contrast with the harmonious and idyllic picture of the mother–child relationship which the ideology of motherhood encourages.[2] In almost all societies, women have the primary parenting functions for children, which reach beyond the biological processes of motherhood, i.e., pregnancy, delivery, and breast feeding. According to the ideology of motherhood, this is a universal and biological fact, but the mother–child relationship and the forms of child care have nevertheless changed considerably across time and place. For example, even within Western European industrial societies there are significant differences between the conditions women as mothers experience. Legislation concerning abortion, maternity (and paternity leave), collective child care provision and child benefits all influence women's reproductive choices and their opportunities to combine mothering with employment.

In this article, I will concentrate on the political aspects of motherhood and mothering, how different countries shape mothering through their legislation and how the limits between public and private are drawn in relation to child care. I concentrate on child care policies because this area influences the responsibility that mothers have for small children very directly. The approach is comparative because an analysis of similarities and differences in child care policies in different countries is one way of evaluating the impact of political decisions on the conditions of motherhood. I focus on the Scandinavian countries and Britain and analyse their child care policies starting with the period during which child care institutions first developed in these countries. The historical approach is important because it seems to me that the continuing similarities and differences between the countries in relation to child care were first established at their very beginnings.

## Theoretical contributions to the understanding of motherhood

The political dimensions of motherhood have only to a very limited degree been the object of scientific investigation compared, for instance, to the psychological dimensions. Psychology has a long and comprehensive tradition of analysing the mother–child relationship which dates back to Freud, and it includes a number of different schools and interpretations. The absence of analysis of motherhood in political science is probably a result of the male domination of this discipline, which is even stronger than in psychology; it is also a reflection of the fact that motherhood is generally perceived and accepted as mainly a biological and psychological phenomenon. Feminists in political science have, however, during the last five to seven years focused increasingly on the significance of motherhood for women's position in society.

The work of the American feminist and political scientist Zillah Eisenstein is an example of this. She focuses on the structural aspects of gender and power and on the role of the state, and she ascribes to motherhood a very central role in the maintenance of the capitalist patriarchy:

> Patriarchy, then, is largely the sexual and economic struggle to control women's options in such a way as to keep primary their role as childbearer and rearer. Power reflects the activity of trying to limit choices. . . . The priorities of patriarchy are to keep the choice limited for woman so that her role as mother remains primary. Patriarchy does not merely exist because men hate women. It exists because as a system of power it provides the mothers of society. This involves the caring and love they provide, the children they reproduce, the domestic labor they do, the commodities they consume, the ghettoized labor force they provide. The starting-point for all these realities is motherhood itself. (Eisenstein, 1983, p. 44)

The problem is not, she argues, that it is women who rear children, but rather 'how this activity becomes assigned within the family and within the larger, social, economic, and political setting' (Eisenstein, 1983, p. 44). In this sense her theory differs from the American sociologist Nancy Chodorow, who discusses 'the reproduction of mothering' (Chodorow, 1979) using a psychological approach. Chodorow also concludes that it is women's primary parenting functions or the fact that women mother which perpetuates male supremacy, but her point is that it is exactly the fact that women rear children and socialize small girls and boys which determines the different sexual identities and roles in society for adults. When men are mothered by women, she argues, it generates a psychology of male dominance and a need to be superior to women. Women, on the other hand, wish to mother and to re-create the triangular relation between mother, father and child which they experienced in their early childhood.

The different approaches of Eisenstein and Chodorow imply disagreements about the fundamental determining factors of patriarchal power. Eisenstein argues that power structures at a society level are the most decisive, and concludes that the state plays a crucial role in controlling women and keeping their mothering role as primary. Chodorow points to the individual and psychological aspects of mothering as fundamental for maintenance of patriarchal power in society. The problem is that neither of them is sufficiently conscious or explicit about the way their respective approaches colour their conclusions. They are both very ambitious about the explanatory power of their theory, in the sense that they claim that it is able to explain patriarchal power as such. An interesting question must be whether the different approaches and theories can be combined in a theory about motherhood and patriarchy.

Another difference between Chodorow and Eisenstein is related to the role they ascribe women and men. Chodorow concentrates on the role of the mother, but her point is parallel to the conclusion of another American feminist, Dorothy Dinnerstein (1976). She argues that the overall dominating power of the mother during early childhood counterbalances male power in society. Patriarchal power is thus maintained because both men and women accept it as a refuge from maternal power. Eisenstein focuses almost unequivocally on male power and the role of men. Thereby she reduces women to objects and makes their role both in preserving and undermining patriarchal power invisible. Although Eisenstein has, in fact, analysed the role of feminism in her empirical work, this has no implications for her theoretical conclusions about the nature and determinants of patriarchy.

The strategical implications of the work of Chodorow, Dinnerstein, and Eisenstein are not very different. They all argue that the unequal power structures between the sexes can be changed if the care of small children becomes more equally shared between fathers and mothers. Dinnerstein and Chodorow both cling to Freudian theory in much of their analysis, but they do not accept the biological determinism that some Freudians advocate. They belong to the so-called object–relation tradition of Freudianism. This relates the psychoanalytic theory and the conclusions of Freud to the specific family structure and the sexual division of work which was dominant in Freud's case material.

If the responsibility for small children is going to be changed, the political dimensions of motherhood become specifically important, and this implies that the work of Zillah Eisenstein becomes interesting also in relation to the psychological theory. She distinguishes between the biological and political dimensions of motherhood in the following way:

> Women can sexually reproduce and they lactate. These are biological facts. That women are defined as mothers is a political fact and reflects the need of patriarchy which is based partially in the biological truth that women bear children. The transformation of women from a biological being (childbearer) to a political being

164    *Anette Borchorst*

(childrearer) is part of a conflict expressed in the politics of patriarchy. Patriarchy seeks to maintain the myth that patriarchal motherhood is a biological reality rather than a political constructed necessity. (Eisenstein, 1981, p. 15)

The political aspects of motherhood are thus related to the way patriarchy seeks to keep the role of women as mothers as primary, and she argues that the state's embodiment of the public and private division aids the process. A serious disadvantage of this analysis (and of Chodorow's and Dinnerstein's analysis as well) is that they all tend to ignore the positive aspects of motherhood and the liberating potential that women derive from it.

In some of the woman-centred analyses which have been made by feminists, these aspects have been more fully explored. The West German sociologist Ulrike Prokop has contributed to a more varied and precise understanding of motherhood in her theory of the context of women's daily life (Prokop, 1976). She argues that womanhood is characterized by ambivalences and ambiguities, because female production forces come into conflict with women's production relations. Among the female production forces, she includes the ability to use need-oriented communication and imagination, and these are, she argues, among other things developed in the mother–child relationship. One of the problems with such a woman-centred perspective is, however, that women's experiences are idealized; moreover, the family is regarded as the central domain for modern women's daily life and the dominant arena for their experiences. In this sense, this approach reproduces both the ideology of motherhood and the concomitant attempts by male political theorists to refer to women only in the private sphere. Thus such theories do not grasp the actual situation of women and their position as working mothers in the same way as Eisenstein does in her work. The analysis of the ambiguities of motherhood is, however, a necessary supplement to Eisenstein's theory.

Zillah Eisenstein argues that the integration of mothers in the labour market gives them potentiality for revolutionary consciousness. It enables them to realize their second-class status more clearly and recognize both patriarchal and capitalist oppression (1981, p. 211; 1983, p. 50). The problem is, however, that political potential and consciousness are only linked to oppression, religion, and a negative concept of power as in the original Marxist interpretation. In contrast, the strength of the women-centred perspective is that it also focuses on the positive values of womanhood and the way in which these positive values empower women to react against patriarchal power.

When one explores the political aspects of motherhood and women's position, the role of the state becomes central in the analysis. Eisenstein also contributes to the project of developing a feminist theory of the state. The role of the state is, she argues, to institutionalize patriarchy and create social cohesion between capitalism and patriarchy. It does this by mediating the conflicts which arise between the interests of class and sex, although at the same time the state has a relative autonomy in relation to the two systems of power. In order to keep women's role as mothers primary, and to control their potential power as reproducers of the species, the state is continually involved in questions of reproductive control and motherhood. Through policies of abortion, contraception, sterilization, pregnancy, disability payments and so forth, the state tries to deny women control over their capacity to reproduce (Eisenstein, 1981, p. 234).

The project of building a theory of how capitalism and patriarchy interact and of pointing out what the role of the state is in this connection is very important. It is also very interesting that Eisenstein ascribes to motherhood such a central significance. However, in my opinion, she over-emphasizes the state as an oppressor of women. One of the problems is, I think, that the theory is generated solely from one state tradition, the liberal American state. Another problem is that the analysis is based on a rather limited historical period, namely the Carter and Reagan administrations. Thus, the question arises as to whether the theory can be applied to other state traditions and to broader historical periods. This does, in fact, imply that one must question whether it, in fact, represents a feminist theory of the state as Eisenstein claims or, more narrowly, is a contribution to the theory building that is going on among feminists recently engaged in welfare state research which looks only at single countries.

In the following I will discuss Eisenstein's conclusions about 'political motherhood' by applying them to the empirical case of child care and child care policies. It is, of course, impossible to generalize upon the entire role of the state by looking at a single policy area, but on the other hand this more limited focus allows us to go much deeper in the analysis. Moreover, child care policy is one of the central areas of the politics of motherhood.

## 1800–1900 The rise of child care institutions

The first child care institutions in Europe were established in the first half of the nineteenth century. Most European countries followed a similar course, but initiatives came first in those countries with the most advanced industrialization process.[3] In Britain, elementary schools, infant schools, and dame schools were established in the first decades of the nineteenth century. In Scandinavia asylums were established around the 1830s, first in Denmark, then in Sweden and Norway. These institutions were often very badly accommodated with very few adults in charge of large numbers of children. The parents of the children who attended such institutions were often poor and could afford only a small fee or paid nothing at all.

These initiatives were usually undertaken by private philanthropists in order to alleviate some of the most disastrous consequences of industrialization and the extension of wage labour. The transition from feudalism to industrialism meant that the family was separated from the means of production and dissolved as a production unit. The care of small children became a major problem for working-class families, because families no longer lived and worked together and were separated from their social and kin network. Fathers, mothers and children above a certain age had to work in factories for many hours a day, and grandparents often lived far away. The limited number of child care institutions which were established in some of the big cities satisfied the need for child care assistance only to a very small degree.

Some decades later, another kind of institution which was aimed at the education of children from upper-class and middle-class families was introduced in many European countries. As a result of the development of the nuclear family, the child began to occupy a new and more significant role in the family, especially in wealthier classes. The concept of childhood was invented, together with new thoughts of the child's development.[4] The German educationist Friedrich Froebel developed ideas about a special type of institution, 'kindergartens', which were rapidly spread all over Europe. He established the first in Germany in 1837. In Britain the first one was started in 1851, in Denmark and Norway this happened in 1870 and in Sweden in 1896. These institutions were small facilities open on a half-day basis. They were staffed by educated professionals, and the costs of administration, accommodation and salaries were mainly covered by the charges paid by the parents. Around the turn of the century, specialized training institutes educating people for Froebelian institutions were established in many countries.

By the turn of the century, the two types of institutions existed in many European countries, although not in any great number. Class distinctions determined which children attended which institutions. The purpose of infant schools was to take *care* of children from working-class families who could not manage that care themselves. The purpose of kindergartens was *educational*, and due to the opening hours and the fees charged for attendance they were mainly used by upper-class and middle-class families. They also relied quite explicitly on a family model in which the mother did not have paid work outside the home.

In many countries efforts were made to spread the educational ideas to institutions for working-class children, but most often these initiatives were quickly abandoned. Most successful were the attempts in Denmark where Froebelian educationists contacted leading Social Democrats in Copenhagen in order to facilitate the cause, and they actually succeeded in establishing a new type of institution, the people's kindergartens (folkebørnehaver), the first of which was opened in 1901. These institutions gradually replaced the infant schools, and thereby the fundamental split between care and education was gradually diminished in Denmark.

It is not legitimate to talk of a specifically *state* policy for child care in this first period of the development of child care institutions. Initiatives were taken by private persons and voluntary organizations in order to provide child care facilities, and class differences were the determinants of the specific outcome of these initiatives. The aim of the institutions was directed either towards the care or the education of children. Froebel's pedagogical ideas relied on a family model in which women did not work outside the family, and infant schools were aimed at families in which the wage labour of women was a necessary evil. Thus child care policies did not in any sense seek to change the situation of women or diminish political motherhood.

## 1900–60 National child care policies are developed

During the decades following the turn of the century, the number of child care facilities increased, although at a very slow rate in all countries. In institutions for working-class children funding represented an enormous problem. Public authorities slowly became involved in regulating conditions concerning the health and the education of the children, and in several countries child care institutions came to be funded by the state budget. In Britain the Maternity and Child Welfare Act of 1918 provided grants for day nurseries and the Education Act for nursery schools the same year. In Denmark the people's kindergartens came to be funded by the state in 1919, although in Norway national support was not given until 1946, but child care institutions had been given local grants since 1840.

It was during this period that policies in the different countries began to diverge. In Britain the distinction between care and education was maintained in state policies, and this was reflected also in the administration and funding of the measures. Nursery schools aimed at education were regulated by the Ministry of Education, whereas day nurseries were administered by the Ministry of Health. Moreover, different groups of professionals were employed in the institutions: nursery schools were staffed by teachers and day nurseries by nursery nurses (Ruggie, 1984). In 1944 the compulsory school age was determined at 5 years, and education was thereby also increased for working-class children.

In Denmark and Sweden, child care policies became integrated with social policy in the 1930s. This was as result of alliances formed between the Social Democratic parties and peasant parties and of their integration into government. In both these countries, child care policies were perceived to be part of a qualitative population policy designed to increase the number of children by improving the health and living standards of families. State subsidies were directed towards institutions for working-class children, and it is noteworthy that child care institutions never became integrated with educational policy as in Britain. Another important difference between Scandinavian countries and Britain is that compulsory school age was 7 in all three countries, and a tradition of teaching children below 6 or 7 years to read and write was never developed in Scandinavia.

In Sweden, in the 1930s the claim for extended public commitment to child care was also linked to the situation of women. Alva
Myrdal, a leading Social Democrat and feminist, took a great
interest in increasing public day care facilities both for the purpose
of alleviating social misery and facilitating women's employment.
She also developed ideas for collectivization of child care in special
institutions, 'storbarnskammare', and together with Gunnar Myrdal and an architect she also proposed collective housing (Myrdal,
1935). These ideas were, however, not put into action on any large
scale.

Alva Myrdal's proposals were widely discussed in the other
Scandinavian countries, but claims for extended public child care
were not to the same degree linked to positive attitudes towards
women's employment in Denmark and Norway. In Denmark,
feminists were actively involved in defending the right of married
women to engage in gainful employment, but they were divided
along class lines on the question of motherhood and child care. The
feminist organizations were dominated by upper-class women, for
whom child care did not represent a great problem because they
normally employed servants in their homes to assist with the house
and care work. When they demanded extension of child care
institutions, it was primarily for the purpose of creating jobs for
their members (Borchorst, 1985, pp. 30–44). Working-class women
demanded child care facilities and legal abortion in order to
diminish the conflicts between paid and unpaid work, but they were
not very well represented at state level and not particularly
numerous at the top level of the Social Democratic party either.
Consequently the interests of working-class women were rarely
defended at the political level.

In Norway, the state began to regulate conditions in child care
institutions later than in the other Scandinavian countries and
subsidies were kept to a minimum. Voluntary and religious
organizations were, however, actively engaged in providing child
care facilities, and the organizations of housewives formed alliances
with professionals in order to promote the cause. The purpose was
to mitigate social misery and provide play facilities for children, but
they did not in any sense intend to encourage women's paid work
outside the family.

In Britain, the state used child care facilities quite consciously as a
means to regulate the supply of female labour during and after the

two world wars. The number of day nurseries increased considerably during the wars and decreased drastically after the wars when the soldiers returned from the front. This did not happen in the Scandinavian countries, partly because they were not actively engaged in warfare, but also because these countries never developed a tradition of using women as a disposable reserve army of labour. After the Second World War, British social policy became widely determined by the ideas of William Beveridge. This meant that legislation became characterized by familism, so that the homemaker–breadwinner family model was supported by giving different social security benefits to women and men, and married and unmarried women (Wilson, 1977). Thus the liberal British state explicitly supported political motherhood.

During the 1950s the number of child care institutions stagnated or declined in all these countries. Ideas about collectivization of child care and house work were discussed at the state level in Denmark and Sweden, but they were never put into action partly because the Cold War created a domestic political climate which was generally hostile to state intervention. In particular, family life was considered a private matter (Borchorst and Siim, 1984). The homemaker–breadwinner family model also became a reality in Scandinavian countries in the sense that the number of housewives increased, although the principle of a 'family wage' never became embedded in the legislation to the extent that it did in Britain.

During this period, all these countries developed national measures for child care, but the responsibility for small children was still overwhelmingly considered to be a private problem and the task of women. Thus state policies took on a rather pragmatic character, underwriting child care provisions only because it was accepted that some mothers had to work. Nevertheless considerable differences between, on the one hand, the British state and, on the other, the Scandinavian states developed, due largely to the domination of government in all the countries of Scandinavia by Social Democratic parties. In Scandinavia the conceptual division between care and education and the differences in provisions for different classes decreased: moreover, these countries did not develop a tradition of purely educational measures for pre-school children. Ideologically there were differences between the way public policies were connected to the situation of women and how the employment of women was perceived. In this respect differences were clearest between the countries of Sweden and Britain: the former expressed at least ideologically positive attitudes towards women's employment, while, during the immediate post-war years, the latter tried explicitly to prevent mothers from engaging in gainful employment.

## 1960 to the present day

During recent years the differences between the British and Scandinavian states have become even clearer. Some of the differences which were created in the first two periods persisted. An example of this is the division between care and education which was maintained in the British child care policy, but which, to all intents and purposes, disappeared in the Scandinavian policies. Other differences were rooted in the very different paths that welfare state development followed in this period.

In Scandinavia, the Social Democratic parties were almost continuously in governmental power during the 1960s and 1970s, and they built up comprehensive welfare states with extensive services provided as universal rights and given without charge, or very low charges compared to actual cost. The welfare services were financed by taxation, and social policy thereby became a tool of equalizing class differences. The underlying principle was that capitalist accumulation was supported, but at the same time the working-class was given compensation for the negative by-products of market forces. Labour and capital gained considerable influence on political decisions through organizational representation at many different levels of the state apparatus. Thereby all the Scandinavian countries gained a distinctly corporatist profile.

Child care policies became part of this welfare state project. In all three countries radical legislative changes were passed in this period. In Denmark this happened in 1965, in Sweden in 1972 and in Norway in 1975. In Denmark and Sweden the reforms resulted in a huge expansion of public child care facilities. The legislation also implied radical changes in forms and objectives of child care provision. All children in Denmark and Sweden became entitled to attend public child care facilities, and public authorities became obliged to provide the places required. Pedagogical objectives were strongly emphasized and play and social contact were regarded as the cornerstones in provision for pre-school children. Terminologically, the designation 'småbørnspæ dagogik' ('pedagogics for small children') was invented, and a new profession of 'småbørnspæ-dagoger' ('pedagogues for small children') was introduced. Education, as distinct from socialization, was perceived as something which was aimed at children above compulsory school age, which in all the Scandinavian countries remained at 7. Voluntary pre-school educational programmes on a part-time basis for 6 year olds were, however, introduced.

In Norway, child care legislation, since 1956 administered by the Ministry of Family and Consumer Affairs (later the Ministry of Consumers Affairs and Government Administration), was built on corresponding ideas, but reform occurred later and did not lead to a similar increase in public commitment to child care (see Leira, this volume). This is due to the later industrialization process in the country and probably also to the fact that the Norwegian Social Democratic Party was out of office from 1965 to 1971. Another explanation for the different Norwegian course is that Norwegian women integrated into the labour market later than Swedish and Danish women.

In Sweden and Denmark the rising demand for labour was a very important motive for the political parties to vote for the child care reforms. Even right-wing parties which regretted the necessity for housewives to work outside their homes supported the reforms. In Denmark the intentions of furthering women's employment were widely discussed in Parliament when the child care reform was passed in the middle of the 1960s, but the law itself was, however, not in any sense related explicitly to the situation of women. In Sweden, child care policies were more explicitly directed towards the situation and employment of women, and there was considerable discussion as to whether child care policies should be directly related to labour market policies. Alva Myrdal was still quite influential at the political level and her ideas about women's position in society were widely discussed among feminists in other countries. At the end of the 1960s, she and Viola Klein suggested a strategy for reconciling employment with motherhood which was totally different from her collectivization proposals in the 1930s (Myrdal and Klein, 1970). Women's employment had become a fact, they maintained, and women were no longer forced to choose between the private and public sphere. Mothers of small children should stay at home and take care of them during the first years, but women could engage in employment before having children and again when the children grew older. They advocated, accordingly, an entirely individualist solution to the contradictions between motherhood and employment and it was based on acceptance of a policy for motherhood. This strategy was also adopted by feminist organizations in Denmark.

Swedish and Danish mothers did in fact solve the problems of combining motherhood with employment individually. The activity rates of married women increased by 20 to 25 per cent during the ten years from 1965 to 1975 in these countries, and among women, mothers of small children reached a relatively high level of employment compared to women without children. Today more than 90 per cent of mothers of small children are in employment in Denmark and Sweden, and this shows that they do not leave the labour market when they have children. A lot of them instead work part-time, and the proportion of part-time working women is higher the more children they have, and the younger the children are. There is general acceptance of the conclusion that the relatively high number of working mothers in Sweden and Denmark is related to the enormous increase in child care facilities during the last thirty years in these countries. Today, coverage by public child care facilities is among the highest in the western world. In 1985, 57 per cent of Danish 2 year olds were enrolled in child care facilities and 69 per cent of the 5 year olds. In Sweden, in 1985, the figures were 51 per cent and 70 per cent respectively.[5]

In neither Britain nor Norway has there been a comparable commitment to the employment of women and to the development of public child care. Nevertheless, married women have become increasingly integrated in the labour force, although there appears to be a time-lag of ten to twenty years compared to the other countries, and the increase has taken place in spite of child care policies rather than because of them. Today more than 60 per cent of Norwegian mothers are in employment compared with 55 per cent of British mothers (HMSO, 1984). Only 12 per cent of the 2 year old Norwegian children and 47 per cent of the 5 year olds are enrolled in public child care facilities. In Britain the coverage is even lower, and there is practically no provision for those under 2 years old. This means that working mothers have to use informal child care solutions such as private child-minders, help from family and relatives and play groups; there are a number of Norwegian mothers who report that they take their children to work (see Arnlaug Leira's chapter in this volume and Leira, 1987).

British child care policies are still determined by the reluctance of the state to intervene in family matters; child care is perceived as a private matter, and, due to the strong ideology of the homemaker–breadwinner family model, the task of women. The distinction between care and education is now so deeply rooted in tradition that it is hardly possible that it will disappear in the years or even decades to come. Tensions between the different branches of administration also prevent attempts to combine the two types of child care (Ruggie, 1984). The difference between the countries has accordingly widened substantially in this period. In Scandinavia, child care became part of the welfare state project of the 1960s and 1970s. A totally new public policy for pre-school children was developed relying on play and social interaction, and was offered to all children regardless of class background. In reality there are differences linked to social background in the actual use of different types of child care institutions; the length of mothers' education has proved to be especially significant in this respect.

This analysis has revealed considerable differences between the Scandinavian countries, and this implies that it is also in this area questionable to operate with a specific Scandinavian model.[6] Norway does in fact in some ways resemble Britain more than Denmark and Sweden. In recent years the development in Sweden and Denmark has also differentiated mainly because the economic crisis has been more severe in Denmark than in Sweden and unemployment much higher. In Denmark cut-backs in public expenditure have occurred in many social service areas and child care provision is one of them. Denmark no longer adheres to original policy intentions of covering the need for child care, and instead charges levied on parents have increased. Finally, Sweden has given more priority to care in the family and increased the responsibility of the father through legislation for paternity leave and absence during sickness of the child. Until now this has, however, not resulted in any great reduction in mothers' ultimate responsibility for the care of their children.

It has been striking that the new feminist movement, which was formed in all the countries in the end of the 1960s and the beginning of the 1970s, has not acted as a strong pressure group in relation to child care. The substantial differences in motherhood conditions which had previously existed between the classes had almost disappeared by this time, but motherhood and child care still seemed to be a controversial issue even among feminists. In the first place, the new feminist movement articulated a strong attack on the traditional role of women, and therefore motherhood and child care were not given much attention. In the middle of the 1970s the woman-centred perspective led to much more focus on motherhood (Eisenstein, 1984), but this did not result in a clearer attitude to the question of motherhood and child care. Extreme strategies were developed, such as Shulamith Firestone's rejection of both biological and political motherhood (Firestone, 1972), and, at the other extreme, the wages-for-housework fraction of the movement which totally accepted women's primary responsibility for child care and housework, but tried to re-evaluate it. Neither of these strategies gained much general support. Accordingly, motherhood and child care have also in this period been issues which have been an object of disagreement and have divided feminists. This has also meant a lack of specific strategies to enable women to overcome contradictions between motherhood and employment/education/political activities. In recent years British feminists such as Denise Riley, Caroline New and Miriam David (Riley, 1983; New and David, 1985) have developed strategies for child care, but otherwise child care has remained a relatively muted political issue among feminists.

## Conclusions

Have child care policies then reduced or preserved the role and ideology of motherhood in Scandinavia and Britain, and what can be concluded about the role of the state?

First of all, a comparative approach has revealed considerable differences between the countries. Britain has quite *explicitly* supported motherhood by a very low commitment to child care and by the familistic character of policies in general. Norway has *implicitly* supported the breadwinner–homemaker family model by keeping public child care provision at a minimum. Sweden and Denmark have *actively* supported the integration of women in the labour force and have had a considerable shift from private to public child care. The question remains whether this has actually reduced 'political motherhood' or whether it has re-emerged in a new form.

In my view, increasing public responsibility for pre-school children has undoubtedly relieved mothers of some of the burden of responsibility and it has contributed to the empowering of women through employment and education in the sense that they have obtained a higher degree of autonomy and independence from husbands and marriage. On the other hand, the responsibility for children still overwhelmingly lies with mothers. Therefore one must distinguish between the *quantitative* and *qualitative* aspects of political motherhood, of which the former has diminished but the latter not to the same degree. I find that especially in Sweden and Denmark, political motherhood has emerged in a new form. A large number of mothers are employed in these countries, but they have enormous problems solving the contradictions between the two kinds of activity which they must tackle individually because the state has not set out to resolve these contradictions. Women have been integrated into a labour market which is structured by a male norm: working conditions, hours of work, and, to a certain degree, wages, have relied on the principle that the 'normal' worker has somebody else to take care of the house and care work within the family. Even when individual fathers and mothers have set out to share the responsibility for small children equally, external norms and economic and social policies in practice support political motherhood. The state still maintains a hierarchical and gendered division of work and it has, by means of child care policies, institutionalized women's double shift.[7] The individual strategy of shared parenting advocated by Chodorow is relatively weak in the face of wide and powerful social, economic and political structures. It is a challenge for women to use the political influence they have obtained in order to undermine these patriarchal structures.

However, this also means that Zillah Eisenstein's contribution to a feminist theory of the state needs further elaboration in several ways. Her conclusions are too much coloured by the fact that they are derived solely from a liberal state tradition. The Scandinavian states, especially during the last twenty to twenty-five years, have developed a more egalitarian child care policy and they cannot simply be characterized as oppressive of women. Eisenstein fails to pay enough attention to factors such as differences in levels of economic development and demand for labour, and largely ignores the influence which persons, groups and organizations have had on the decision-making process in different countries. The task of feminists in different countries remains twofold: firstly to develop strategies which are sensitive to their own political systems and which are designed to remove the patriarchal state's control of the conditions of motherhood, while secondly, and at a more general level, to develop a vision of the actualities of motherhood which preserves its most positive aspects.

## Notes

1. See S. Sharpe (1984), A. Borchorst and B. Siim (1984), C. Kugelberg (1987), and A. Leira in this volume.
2. See A. Dally (1982), and A. Oakley (1974, pp. 185–222).
3. The following relies on: N. Whitbread (1972) and J. Tizard, P. Moss and J. Perry (1976) for Britain; A. Borchorst and B. Siim (1984) for Denmark; G. Kyle (1979) for Sweden; and J. A. Lea (1982) for Norway.
4. See, for example, P. Ariés (1962), E. Shorter (1977), and E. Badinter (1982).
5. Statistical comparisons between child care in different countries are complicated by different length of maternity leave and programmes for pre-school activities. Also, different methods of counting complicate the picture, even between Scandinavian countries. Therefore I have chosen age groups for which comparison is valid. See L. Togeby (1987).
6. For a comparison between contemporary child care policies in Scandinavia see A. Leira (1987).
7. See A. Borchorst and B. Siim (1987).

## References

Ariés, P. (1962), *Centuries of Childhood* (London: Penguin)
Badinter, E. (1982), *The Myth of Motherhood* (London: Souvenir Press)
Borchorst, A. (1985), 'Barnomsorg och Kvinnokrav', in *Kvinnovetenskaplig tidsskrift*, no. 6
Borchorst, A. and Siim, B. (1984), *Kvinder i velfærdsstaten – mellem moderskab og lønarbejde gennem 100 år* (Aalborg, Denmark: Aalborg University Press)
Borchorst, A. and Siim, B. (1987), 'Women and the advanced welfare state – a new kind of patriarchal power?' in A. Showstack Sassoon (ed.), *Women and the State* (London: Hutchinson)

Chodorow, N. (1979), *The Reproduction of Mothering* (Berkeley: University of California Press)

Dally, A. (1982), *Inventing Motherhood* (London: Burnett Books)

Dinnerstein, D. (1976), *The Mermaid and the Minotaur* (New York: Harper Colophon Books)

Eisenstein, Z. (1981), *The Radical Future of Liberal Feminism* (New York: Longman)

Eisenstein, Z. (1983), 'The state, the patriarchal family and working mothers', in I. Diamond (ed.), *Families, Politics and Public Policy* (New York: Longman)

Eisenstein, Z. (1984), *Contemporary Feminist Thought* (London and North Sydney: Unwin Paperbacks)

Firestone, S. (1972), *The Dialectics of Sex* (London: Paladin)

HMSO (1984), *Women and Employment. A Life Time Perspective* (London: Her Majesty's Stationery Office)

Kugelberg, C. (1987), *Allt eller inget* (Stockholm: Carlssons)

Kyle, G. (1979), 'Gästarbetarska i manssamhället' (Stockholm: Liber Förlag)

Lea, J. A. (1982), *Framveksten av norsk barnhagepolitikk* (Oslo: Institutt for anvendt sosialvitenskaplig forskning (NAS 82:12))

Leira, A. (1987), *Day Care in Denmark, Norway and Sweden* (Oslo: Institutt for Samfunnsforskning)

Myrdal, A. (1935), *Stadsbarn* (Stockholm: KF Förlag)

Myrdal, A. and Klein, V. (1970), *Women's Two Roles* (London: Routledge and Kegan Paul)

New, C. and David, M. (1985) *For the Children's Sake* (Harmondsworth: Penguin)

Oakley, A. (1974), *Housewife* (London: Penguin Books)

Prokop, U. (1976), *Kvindelig livssammenhaeng* (Randers: GMT)

Riley, D. (1983), 'The serious burdens of love? Some questions on child care, feminism and socialism', in L. Segal (ed.) *What is to be done about the family?* (Harmondsworth: Penguin)

Ruggie, M. (1984), *The State and Working Women* (New Jersey: Princeton University Press)

Sharpe, S. (1984), *Double Identity* (Harmondsworth: Penguin)

Shorter, E. (1977), *The Making of the Modern Family* (Glasgow: Fontana)

Tizard, J., Moss, P. and Perry, J. (1976), *All Our Children* (London: Temple Smith/New Society)

Togeby, L. (1987), *Notat om børnepasningsdaek ningen i de nordiske lande* (University of Aarhus: Institute of Political Science)

Whitbread, N. (1972), *The Evolution of the Nursery–Infant School* (London: Routledge and Kegan Paul)

Wilson, E. (1977), *Women and the Welfare State* (London: Tavistock)

CHAPTER 9

# CONCLUSION

## CLARE UNGERSON

The purpose of this concluding chapter is twofold. First I wish to draw together the two main strands of this book, namely the topic concerned with the care of normal children, particularly those of pre-school age, and the topic of caring for dependent elderly people, and to consider how far it is useful to think about these two activities together. As has already been mentioned (Chapter 1), there was some puzzlement on both sides of the linguistic and geographical divide as to why a conference on 'Cross-national perspectives on gender and community care' should bring together, on the part of the Scandinavian participants, both child care analysts and commentators on the care of the dependent elderly, whereas, amongst the British participants, the term 'caring' had come to have a much narrower and more specific meaning, referring to the care of the incapacitated only.

The other major theme of the book is the political context within which policies for women have developed, particularly in the Scandinavian countries, and it is this theme which leads into the second purpose of this brief concluding chapter – namely, to draw attention to the way in which the political climate as regards mothering is very rapidly changing in Britain today as policy-makers and businessmen (the masculine used advisedly here) increasingly, and in public, express their anxiety at a potential labour shortage problem now named – in Britain – 'the demographic time-bomb'.

179

## Children and the dependent elderly: different or the same?

Of course these two demographic groups are different. It seems absurd to subsume into the same category ignorance and knowledge, anticipation and biography, potential growth and actual decline. And yet, when it comes to considering highly dependent old age, Shakespeare's 'second childhood' still has a telling salience. Both groups are in need of someone to care for them and protect them from the world's exigencies.

However, I shall tackle the differences first. In the case of infants and children, the person or people responsible for providing that care are, as a result of the social organization of most of the developed world, almost always taken to be the biological parents, with the mother playing the much more central and crucial role. There are two conceptual elements to the basis for this norm: these are naturalism, which maintains that social relationships spring from biological relationships, and essentialism, which claims that the best people to maintain these bio/social relationships are women because they, as a sex, contain a specially appropriate set of attributes for mothering. Moreover, the fact that social parenting is allied so closely to biological parenting and regarded as the norm, endows such parenting with a special legitimacy which is maintained by the political and judicial system: parents and children are treated as though they 'belong' to each other. (An obvious example is the right of children to migrate to their parents in Britain; blood testing is commonly used to establish such biological links.) However, such firmly established legitimacy is not so clear when it comes to responsibility for the care of elderly kin. Indeed, an important part of the current debate about 'community care' is precisely the argument about how far government and government agencies can expect biologically related kin to take full responsibility for the care of dependents who are not their own children. The argument is at its fiercest and most murky when it comes to whether or not adult children have full responsibility for the care of their own parents. It seems to me that naturalism and essentialism are not – not yet at any rate – fully established as the great bed-rocks on which the care of the elderly can be placed. The argument will, no doubt, continue well into the next century. In Britain at the moment hardly a day passes without some serious media attention covering the problems of an individual household in coping with the care of dependent kin.

Both sides use, as best they can, whatever arguments opportunistically come to hand. For example, the recent debates about the extent and management of incestuous child sexual abuse has, in Britain, put a question mark against the 'naturalness' of bio-social parenting, which may well be used by those wishing to undermine naturalistic arguments elsewhere.

A second important difference between caring for dependent people other than children and caring for normal children is the question of development, and its complement, the process of socialization. Moreover, it is precisely this question which, in turn, legitimizes the intervention of the state in the process of child development, even where naturalism and essentialism – as I have argued in the previous paragraph – very strongly prevail. As far as elderly dependent people are concerned, their development and growth are assumed to be largely over and, in post-industrial societies, so too are their labour and labour market utility. The state has only very limited interests in intervening in the care of elderly people. For example, one of the chief purposes of professionalized services for elderly dependent people is not so much to develop their capacities and talents further but to find and promulgate techniques of *retaining* their existing faculties, in order to minimize their dependence on other state-provided services.

However, normal children are clearly in the process of growth and development, moreover, it is in the interests of state and society to ensure that children's talents are groomed for successful integration into the adult world of social cohesion and paid work. Hence state intervention in the process of child socialization is not nearly so open to question as it is *vis-à-vis* other dependent people. Indeed, as far as children are concerned, the debate in Europe has, since the second half of the nineteenth century, been not so much *whether* the state should intervene in the process of child development but *at what age*. Different nations come to different conclusions about the appropriate starting age for compulsory education, with the Scandinavians, as with most of the rest of Europe, having a school-starting age at least a year behind the British. However, pre-school care organized by the state can also, within this framework of the acknowledged necessity of child socialization beyond the family, very easily be justified on a proto-universalist scale. In Britain we lag behind the Scandinavians in using such an argument, the naturalist and, more particularly, the essentialist arguments about mothering of pre-school children being far and away pre-eminent. But, even in this country, an earlier compulsory school age (5 years compared, for example, to the Swedish starting age of 7) goes some way to acknowledging the strength of the socialization arguments. In developed societies, the first day at school, even when accompanied by tears, is treated as one of life's inevitable *rites de passage*; in contrast, the weeping granny in her first six weeks at the residential home is usually pitied and her relatives regarded as somewhat lacking in care and attention. In other words, the role of the state *vis-à-vis* child care is generally settled, although arguments continue to rage – based on naturalism and essentialism – as to the point in infancy and childhood at which such intervention should occur. But as far as elderly people are concerned, where socialization and social control are not the issues, the case for state intervention and state responsibility *per se* is now the subject of long and hard debate.

Perhaps these differences are somewhat exaggerated, because it is also clear that, when it comes to caring of all kinds, the debates about the relative responsibilities of state, kin, and community also have a great deal in common. Their most common feature is the gendered nature of the language of the debate, with the assumption almost always being made that, as far as child care is concerned, it is the mothers who are at the centre of the issue, and as far as other carers are concerned, it is more than likely that such carers will be female. Moreover, feminist critiques of this gendered division of labour throw into question the way such care in the private domain is to be costed and accounted for when it comes to decision-making about efficient use of resources, and how far caring can be construed as 'work'. From this follow the debates about remuneration and recognition for carers and domestic labourers (discussed at length in my chapter in this volume). In addition, the gendered nature of caring – for whatever kind of dependant and dependency – throws into relief a debate about where women's responsibility ends and not just the state's but also *men's* responsibility begins. And here again the role of the state can be to try to orchestrate a changing sexual division of labour, by, for example, introducing parental rather than maternity leave – as in Sweden. Finally, both caring for dependent elderly people and caring for children raise the question of where high-quality care can be most appropriately provided. For each there is a trichotomy of care: care at home by biologically related kin, care at home by others, or care elsewhere, on a daily or residential basis, with only a limited amount of contact with, and care by, kin. At the moment, debates about the merits of, for example, communal provision for infants and children and similar provision for other dependent people tend to take place without reference to each other – but there are clearly parallels and insights that can be drawn from discussion about forms of provision which are presently assumed to be suited to one group but that may well be suited to others.

## The politics of caring and the 'demographic time-bomb'

One way in which caring for children and caring for elderly dependent people can be put together is demonstrated by an illuminating policy discussion that is developing in Britain at the moment. The context for this discussion is the treatment of women primarily as *workers*, but also as cai ers. In this context, the discussion of caring is confined to how the caring responsibilities of women of working age can be dispersed and carried out by others during the conventional working day. The debate has been initiated by a predicted labour shortage. Articles and reports published by government departments and agencies during 1988 made much of a projected decline in the numbers of school-leavers available for entry into the British labour market: between 1987 and 1995 the number of such potential young recruits is expected to reduce by 1.2 million, or 23 per cent (National Economic Development Office, 1988; Department of Employment, May 1988).[1] At the same time, an important comparative study of child care facilities in the member states of the EC was also published (Cohen, 1988). This report indicated that the level of provision for the care of pre-school children in Britain was one of the lowest in Europe; the Danes, for example, spend six times more of their GNP on pre-school provision. During 1989, there has been increasing public attention paid to the issue, and it has been named by the national media the 'demographic time-bomb'.

The impact of these reports and concern has brought together a coalition of political actors, one of the most important of which is the Equal Opportunities Commission (a government funded agency charged with securing and monitoring the progress of sex equality in Britain). At the beginning of 1989 the EOC launched its new strategy for 1989–93; the first of its 'themes and objectives' was announced as follows:

> Making the most of human resources, in an era of skills shortage and demographic change, means looking to women; our first theme is 'work and the family'.

> To make it easier for women – and men – to be effective and responsible employees and effective and responsible family members.

> *Objectives*
> 1. To persuade employers to provide support for working parents and other carers.
> 2. To establish good practice models for out-of-school care and holiday schemes for children aged 5–13.
> 3. To achieve improved status, qualifications and training for childminders and similar child care workers.
> 4. To enhance the status of part-time work and to achieve for part-time workers pay and non-pay benefits equivalent to those of full-timers. (EOC News Release, January 17, 1989)

In March 1989 the EOC, in conjunction with the Confederation of British Industry (the most powerful national representative of employers' interests and very largely in support of present Conservative government policies), set about its first strategic aim and held a widely reported national conference on 'Work and the Family'. Norman Fowler, Secretary of State for Employment, Norman Willis, General Secretary of the Trades Union Congress, Sir Trevor Holdsworth, President of the CBI, and Sir Archibald Forster, Chairman of Esso plc, gave plenary addresses. As Joanna Foster, Chair of the EOC, put it:

> Today's conference is attended by organizations who are concerned about their competitive edge and their future resourcing; concerned about how to attract in, attract back, train and retain more of the best possible people as their employees, taking into account that 80 per cent of the new jobs in the next five years will be filled by women the majority of whom will have major family responsibilities . . . the arguments about who should or could provide what sort of child care are rife and 'eldercare' is also entering the discussions, along with other 'cafeteria-style' perks for full-time and *pro rata* benefits for

part-time workers. . . . These initiatives are welcome but are still happening in very few organizations. They are provoked not by employer altruism or a change in heart about moral responsibilities or social justice, it is enlightened self-interest. (Foster, March 1989)

The purpose of the conference was clear: it was, as the EOC had said in their strategic policy document, to persuade *employers* that it was they (not the government) who faced a problem and that their profits were at risk unless they (and not the government) took immediate action. Norman Fowler, Secretary of State for Employment, made a speech entitled 'The Rights of Women' in which, in almost every paragraph, he referred to the responsibility of employers to provide facilities that would encourage recruitment of mothers:

> Employers will need to adapt their traditional working practices to accommodate the needs of women as well as the needs of men. That means above all greater flexibility. It means flexibility in hours of work and in holidays to allow working mothers to take care of children outside school hours. It means a willingness to explore the scope for home-working. It means that more employees will provide child care facilities . . . . Flexibility also means that employers need to expand the scope for job sharing and part-time working . . . I do not underestimate the challenge this will pose to traditional ways of organizing work and structuring jobs. But the message of demographic change is clear. Those employers who are not prepared to adapt, to retrain and to look beyond their traditional areas of recruitment will find that their businesses cannot grow and compete in the 1990s. (Fowler, March 1989)

There were two slightly dissenting voices: Sir Trevor Holdsworth, the CBI's President, at the end of what was an equally exhortatory speech to employers, requested that the government lift the tax on employees who use workplace crêches (a piece of policy which, despite its tiny revenue implications of £1 million, has not been enacted) (Holdsworth, 1989). Norman Willis of the TUC, meanwhile, said that 'flexibility' would only be acceptable if it improved trade unionists' lives and not if it meant 'allowing members' rights to be undermined in the name of flexibility' (Willis, 1989).

I have dwelt at length on this conference because it seems to me to illustrate very well the considerable differences between policy assumptions and policy ends in the countries of Scandinavia, on the one hand, and in Britain on the other. In the first place, we have here an expressed concern with a potential labour shortage being allied to the idea that women, particularly mothers, can be used to fill the labour shortage so long as some aspects of mothering – particularly the need to look after pre-school children during the working day – can be taken over by another agency, or that the impact of mothering can be reduced by introducing special 'career break' leaves and shortening the working day. This has clear parallels with the development of pre-school child care in both Denmark and Norway (Borchorst; Leira; both in this volume) particularly during the 1960s. But there the parallels end. In Britain, the present government has made it clear that there will be no state intervention, let alone state provision, to provide for the entry and retention of mothers in the paid labour market. Instead, the government proposes to rely on 'market forces' and persuade employers that they risk losing their 'competitive edge' if they fail to introduce facilities for women. The clearest statement of the government's intention to leave well alone has recently come in two forms: first, a late proposal, now embodied in the Children's Bill currently going through Parliament, that private nurseries and child-minders should be deregulated; and, secondly, the widely publicized decision, endorsed by Margaret Thatcher herself, that the UK should be the only EC member-state not to support a draft European resolution on work and the family (included within the so-called Social Charter) which would encourage 'the sharing of family and occupational responsibilities' and additional provision for pre-school children. Some might argue that the fact that government, the employers and the Equal Opportunities Commission have found a forum to discuss these matters, indicates an embryonic 'corporatism' along Scandinavian lines, but the reliance by the Secretary of State on exhortation and threats of economic decline alone indicates, again, that government in Britain has no intention of subsidizing enterprise initiative in this area, let alone creating direct state funded and managed provision.

Thus services particularly for mothers but also for other carers, despite government concern about possible labour market shortages, are being kept firmly out of the political arena in Britain. This is in marked contrast to the countries of Scandinavia, where, with the same initial impulsion, child care has become a matter of high priority in state policy and public expenditure. But before running away with the assumption that, if only the British government were to subsidize employers, this would be enough, it is important to make four further crucial points. First, these government exhortations do not constitute a policy about caring, second, this is not a policy about women, third, this is an easily reversed set of exhortations, and, finally, if provision develops, such services can only be defended within the economic rather than the political arena, and on opportunistic grounds rather than on the grounds of rights of citizenship generally and women's rights in particular.

It is clear this is not a policy about caring which is designed to relieve the carers of children and of other dependent people of the responsibility for full-time care. This is especially demonstrated where children are concerned by the talk of provision of workplace nurseries, with apparently no discussion as to whether such a location is the best place for the care of children (the mere idea of carrying infants to work on the London Underground . . .!). In other words, no thought apparently is being given to the question of the quality of this replacement care – a matter with which carers are continuously concerned. This leads on to my second point: namely, that this is not a 'women's policy' – it is a 'working mothers' policy'. It will provide women with relief from caring only if they are also in paid work; thus women outside conventional working ages, and women who are not in paid work, are to be excluded from such caring relief should it occur. Nevertheless, there are clearly opportunities here for women of working age to place pressure on their employers. Unfortunately, the fact that such pressure is at present being orchestrated by a government which is simultaneously dismantling regulation of private nurseries, and consistently refusing to go along with the extension of women's rights through EC legislation resolutions and directives, is a clear sign that women's interests are very far from being directly addressed. Thirdly, the policy is completely reversible precisely because it is being presented as a solution to a short-term crisis: the so-called demographic time-bomb. The forthcoming labour shortage is being presented and discussed almost as though this is 1939 rather than 1989; even the militaristic language provides a distant echo of wartime. As was evident in Britain after the Second World War, even where government is heavily involved in provision for child care and family meals, such a provision can be disbanded with relative ease once the short-term situation is 'resolved'. Thus, given the language with which the present situation is being described, there is no reason why, if employers are persuaded to invest in child care provision on a mass scale, such provision should not decline to practically nothing once they consider that the demographic and economic moment has passed. Moreover, in this particular case, it is highly likely that the close-down will be even easier than in the aftermath of the Second World War, since any defence of the provision will have to be mounted through the arena of the workplace rather than the polity. When the time comes, a weakened trade union movement that has, in the past, fought men's rather than women's battles is hardly likely to mount a totally successful defence of women's working conditions.

Finally, such changes in provision, should they occur, are not being conducted within the context of a re-appraisal of the rights of women in general, or those of carers in particular. It is here that the starkest contrast between Britain, on the one hand, and the Scandinavian countries (particularly Denmark and Sweden) on the other, arises. For in those countries, despite problems outlined in the papers in this volume, there has, in the past twenty years, been a fundamental shift in thinking: care within and by the 'family' is no longer regarded as necessarily the epitome of high-quality care – indeed, particularly for pre-school children, it is argued that children are advantaged if they attend day care away from their parents. Moreover, these governments are, on the whole, interventionist in terms of provision (although the amount and direction of that intervention vary from country to country). They attempt to pursue gender-free policies, but understand that, in order for such policies to work, the social relations between men and women must be changed so that the domestic division of labour is made more equal. They also realize that government has a responsibility to provide the legislative framework that assists, rather than hinders, such change in the relations between the sexes.

However, the situation is not so advantageous to women, even in the countries of Scandinavia, when it comes to caring for the elderly, as Kari Wærness's chapter in this volume makes clear. And this brings us back to the point made in the previous section of this conclusion. The discussion about where and when the state has a duty and responsibility to intervene in the care of those dependent people who are not normal children has a strength and a universality which is far stronger than the similar debates about the role of the state in the care and socialization of children alone. Although I have

argued that naturalism and essentialism are a weaker context for the
care of elderly people than they are for the care of pre-school
children, when it comes to the care of elderly people these two
concepts have a clear field, unhindered by any consideration of
socialization or social control. At present, in Britain at least, labour
market needs may help shift the balance a little, but more for
mothers than for other women carers, since many of the latter will
themselves be of an age considered 'too old' for labour market
utility (although apparently perfectly capable of carrying out the
responsibility for full-time caring at home). I have argued that if a
policy is to work in the interests of all women, irrespective of their
age, and whether or not they are carers or cared for, then the
Scandinavian example shows that the need for women to work in
the paid labour market may provide an impulsion towards the
development of public services to relieve and substitute for carers.
But such an initiating impulse will be far from adequate since it will
only assist carers of working age. It is therefore essential that
policies which are woman-centred develop, rather than policies that
are paid worker centred, but this hangs crucially on the ability of
mothers and carers to insert their needs and rights into the political
as well as the economic process.

## Notes

1. It is remarkable that no publicity had been given before to this 'shortage'
   – predictable since 1973. One can only assume that the silence about it
   reflected a government hope that, if unemployment continued to be a
   problem into the 1990s, then this decrease in the number of school-
   leavers could be used as a device to present unemployment as in decline.

## References

Cohen, B. (1988), *Caring for children: Services and Policies for Childcare
    and Equal Opportunities in the United Kingdom* (Brussels: Commission
    of the European Communities)
Department of Employment (1988), 'New entrants to the labour market',
    *Employment Gazette*, 96, no. 5, May

Equal Opportunities Commission (1989), *News Release*, January 17, (London: EOC)

Foster, J. (1989), *Extracts from the speech by Joanna Foster, Chair of the Equal Opportunities Commission, at the 'Work and the Family' Conference held on 2 March 1989 at the Queen Elizabeth Conference Hall in London* (London: mimeo, obtainable from EOC Press Office)

Fowler, N. (1989), *The Rights of Women*, speech made at the joint EOC/CBI conference on 'Work and the Family', *op. cit.*

Holdsworth, T. (1989), *Keeping our competitive edge – the need for Britain to respond to change*, speech made at the joint EOC/CBI conference on 'Work and the Family', *op. cit.*

National Economic Development Office and Training Commission (1988), *Young People and the Labour Market* (London: NEDO)

Willis, N. (1989), *The changing needs of a changing workforce – speech outline*, speech made at the joint EOC/CBI conference on 'Work and the Family', *op. cit.*

# INDEX

*The abbreviations f, n, and t refer to figure, note and table, respectively.*